Social Media

Claudia Wyrwoll

Social Media

Fundamentals, Models, and Ranking of User-Generated Content

Foreword by Prof. Dr. Horst Oberquelle

 Springer Vieweg

Claudia Wyrwoll
Hamburg, Germany

Doctoral Thesis, Universität Hamburg, Germany, 2014

ISBN 978-3-658-06983-4   ISBN 978-3-658-06984-1 (eBook)
DOI 10.1007/978-3-658-06984-1

The Deutsche Nationalbibliothek lists this publication in the Deutsche Nationalbibliografie;
detailed bibliographic data are available in the Internet at http://dnb.d-nb.de.

Library of Congress Control Number: 2014946897

Springer Vieweg
© Springer Fachmedien Wiesbaden 2014

Printed on acid-free paper

Springer Vieweg is a brand of Springer DE.
Springer DE is part of Springer Science+Business Media.
www.springer-vieweg.de

To Dr. Kai Stietenroth,

who taught me anything can be done.
He went out and made the world a better place.
He is painfully missed. And always will be.

Foreword

When Carl Adam Petri, the father of Petri Nets, entitled his PhD Thesis "Communication with Automata" in 1962, almost no one understood that the computer was on its way to become a new medium. This title had two interpretations: interaction with computers can be understood as a special form of communication: human-computer communication. This view has influenced my professional life when becoming a specialist in usability. The other interpretation is: people communicate via computers. In 1962 a bold vision. But the technical basis for this view was already on its way: the concept for a computer network was published in the same year by Joseph C. R. Licklider (the author of "Man-Computer Symbiosis"—the first interpretation) and others. This work on packet-switched networks led to the ARPA-Net and finally to the Internet. Scientists used this network since 1970. Networked computers became the norm. The topic of computer-supported cooperative work with new problems of usability emerged. This became my second field of interest. A leading question was: how can we design computer applications in such a way that users can understand and use them easily?

The publicly available Internet is now with us for 25 years, often considered identical with the World Wide Web (WWW). Since Tim Berners-Lee published the first web browser in 1992, the WWW evolved into a complete new medium used by everybody. The overwhelming mass of information asked for new ways of accessing. Search engines like Google were the answer 16 years ago. Meanwhile it has become normal to "google" an answer for any kind of question. In many cases very successfully.

The Internet enabled not only the distribution of information provided by specialists, it allowed to implement new services which were called Web 2.0, services which enable anyone to be author and reader. New platforms emerged which are called social media: blogs, forums, media sharing platforms, social networks, etc. The daily reality of many people is governed by Google, Facebook, Twitter, and the like. These platforms provide an unbelievable amount of user-generated content to the public. Surprisingly, there are almost no tools to exploit the richness of this information. Current search engines are not adequate, since their basic unit of search is a web page while social media have a different granularity. For collecting and ranking user-generated content across social media platforms there was no solution before Claudia Wyrwoll started her PhD-work three years ago.

The publication of her results shows that this difficult problem can be solved exploiting the meta-data provided by social media. I am convinced that her concept can be the basis for a new generation of user-adequate tools for the exploitation of the richness of information contained and provided in social media.

Hamburg   Prof. Dr. Horst Oberquelle

Acknowledgments

I am grateful to have had the opportunity to undertake the studies this work documents. My advisers Prof. Dr. Horst Oberquelle and Prof. Dr. Christopher Habel gave me the freedom to self-determinedly follow my research goals while always being on the spot when I needed advice. I am profoundly grateful to Prof. Dr. Horst Oberquelle for supporting my efforts during the whole time and shoring me up when I doubted myself. I thank him for his advice, his patience and his empathy. I thank Prof. Dr. Christopher Habel for his thoughtful feedback which helped to increase structural and verbal clarity of the text. I thank my friends and colleagues Philip Joschko and Dr. Johannes Göbel for discussing ideas with me and helping me through all of Latex' contumacies. I thank my parents for the liberty to start for where ever I like and do whatever I love. Last but not least, I thank Christian Wyrwoll for encouraging me in everything I do.

Contents

List of Figures

List of Tables

1 Introduction

> *The Web was originally supposed to be a personal information system and a tool for groups of all sizes, from a team of two to the entire world.*
>
> Tim Berners-Lee (1996, p. 69)

The Web revolutionized communication twice. First, when it was invented, and second, when social media enabled people, who are no computer specialists, to make content publicly available to other users. Earlier broadcasting media could not be used by private individuals to broadcast their thoughts. Figure 1.1 illustrates how people could reach unacquainted others before the advent of social media.

The possibility for everyone to easily publish and share content with the public through the World Wide Web has changed communication. Social media has transformed mass communication from the monopoly of the unidirectional communication medium of the traditional mass media (i.e., printing press, television and radio) to multidirectional communication where everyone can participate. Social media facilitated a shift from a consume-oriented communication culture to a communication culture of participation. A world in which a small number of people report, create, decide, and form opinions is developing into a world in which everyone has opportunities to actively participate (Fischer, 2011). The advantages of this are manifold.

Content created by users and made publicly available online becomes an alternative news source. In combination with the last decade's achievements in hardware development, equipping a huge part of the world with mobile devices with camera and mobile access to the Internet, anyone could be the one to post something as it happens making it news, if only enough others consider it relevant. The possibility for everyone to create content and make it publicly available also empowers civil rights movements, because it is not as easily controlled and censored as centralized traditional mass media. The possibility for consumers to connect and share their experiences and grievances facilitates ethical consumerism. Consumer-generated content enervates the power of marketing communications. It also becomes a new source for market research.

And as more people participate, more content is created, shared and available. The social network Facebook (2013) counts 1.15 billion monthly active users as of June 2013. The microblogging service Twitter has "well over 200 million active users creating over 400 million Tweets each day" (Wickre, 2013). 100 hours of video are uploaded to YouTube every minute (Youtube, 2013). The blogging platform Tumblr hosts 141.1 million blogs with 63.8 billion content units available (Tumblr, 2013b).

As more content is created at higher frequency, new challenges arise. Already in 1945, long before the success of the Internet, Bush (1945, p. 38) pointed out that there is too much information to make use of it: "The difficulty seems to be not so much that we publish unduly in view of the extent and variety of present day interests, but rather that publication has been extended far beyond our present day ability to make real use of the record." The rapidly growing volume of information available online makes it increasingly difficult for users to find what they are looking for. From the tremendous amount of information available users need to find information and then evaluate it. In the context of social media, users are not only interested in content that refers to a specific topic. Independent of the topic, users may be interested in criteria such as the popularity of user-generated

Figure 1.1: Speakers' Corner.
The Speakers' Corner is a place of free speech. Before arrival
of Internet and social media, this was the only possibility
that private individuals, who do not happen to be journalists
and do not have a publisher, could reach people they did not
know. This photo shows John Webster addressing a crowd of
listeners in front of the Art Gallery in Sydney. Photo taken
by R. Skobe, 1964 (Zammit, 2008).

content. Search engines based on query-dependent ranking support users insufficiently in this task, because they have two major weaknesses: they require the user to specify a search term and they neglect the specifics of user-generated content.

Currently, users can evaluate content by consuming and judging the value of the content. Furthermore, various types of additional information is available as metadata that can be used to classify content. An example are ratings by other users. Unfortunately, users have to analyze this information manually. For the majority of users it is therefore a major problem to distinguish good from bad results (Jansen, Zhang & Zhang, 2007; Keane, O'Brien & Smyth, 2008). Finding and classifying content is therefore an often time consuming research process. Statistics and rankings, if available, are platform-specific. Users have no possibility to compare contributions from different platforms.

For computer science, the challenge is to develop solutions that support users in the task of coping with the massive amount of data across platforms. A solution that allows to compare user-generated content from different platforms and allows to establish a ranking among them based on the additional information users evaluate manually, can help users in the selection and evaluation process. The goal of this work is to develop a solution that allows to compare and rank user-generated content across platforms by exploiting the information that can be derived from the metadata.

This gives rise to the problem that user-generated content units are difficult to compare, because the number and type of available metadata differs among platforms. There are many different metadata that can be used by users to judge content. Some of which are commonly provided for every type of user-generated content. Others are specific to a certain social media type. These metadata have neither been collected nor classified yet.

Page, Brin, Motwani & Winograd (1998) saw themselves confronted with a similar problem. The World Wide Web grew fast and they searched for a new solution to retrieve relevant Web pages, which they considered to be extremely diverse. They proposed a query-independent link-based ranking approach for Web pages. Link-based approaches that perform well on the task of ranking Web pages do not suffice for user-generated content. User-generated content requires a different level of granularity. Because one Web page can contain more than one user-generated content unit. Furthermore, the additional information that is available for user-generated content—but not for Web pages—remains unutilized.

Related work can be located in two fields of research. First of all, information retrieval, which addresses the problem of retrieval and ranking. Information retrieval offers query-dependent as well as query-independent methods. The subject matters of these methods range from plain text documents to Web pages. Secondly, there is a relatively new research community that addresses the automated analysis of user-generated content. Research goals range from quantifying quality of user-generated content from Wikipedia to identifying high quality answers from Yahoo Answers (Anderka, Stein & Lipka, 2011a; Agichtein, Castillo, Donato, Gionis & Mishne, 2008). Existing research for automated rating and ranking of user-generated content focuses on platform-specific approaches. From a user's point of view, platform-specific approaches have the disadvantage that they do not allow to compare content from different platforms. With platform-specific approaches it is not possible to gain an overview over content from several platforms.

The focus of this work is on query-independent ranking. This has several reasons. First of all, query-independent ranking allows the user to discover content without requiring him to specify a search topic. Secondly, query-dependent ranking has been studied thoroughly. Information retrieval provides several well-established methods for query-dependent ranking. Known approaches for query-dependent ranking can be applied to texts from user-generated content similarly as they are applied to other texts. Furthermore, there are also several known approaches to combine query-dependent with query-independent ranking (Craswell, Robertson, Zaragoza & Taylor,

2005). Thus, the focus on query-independent ranking still allows to combine it with query-dependent ranking, if desired.

In the field of information retrieval we can differentiate between global and personalized search (Marchionini & Shneiderman, 1988). Personalized search systems use personal information about a user's search history and habits to re-rank the search results according to the user's interests and preferences (Ahn & Brusilovsky, 2009). A considerable amount of recent work about search engines focuses on the possibilities to personalize search results, assuming that the user can be served better if preferences, interests and search history are known to the system (e.g., Wang, He, Chang, Song, White & Chu, 2013; Kim, Rawashdeh & El Saddik, 2011; Shen, Tan & Zhai, 2005). Personalization applies a pool of techniques aimed to improve search by taking advantage of the user's preferences. This work explicitly excludes personalized search due to several reasons. It has to be considered that users do not only benefit from personalized search. When people form attitudes, those are assembled from believes about the object's characteristics, feelings and emotions about it and information about past and current actions toward the object. Accessible information dominates attitude judgments (Smith, 2007). If users only find what pleases them, this holds the risk of creating the illusion of an artificially noncontroversial world, in which users only see the section of the world that conforms to their interests and opinions. Personalized search approaches generate search results that tend to confirm the user's opinions and views instead of delivering the results that represent a realistic distribution of opinions. Pariser calls this phenomenon the **filter bubble.** The filter bubble, that results from personalized search, holds personal and cultural threads. It surrounds users with ideas with which they are already familiar making them overconfident in their mental frameworks. Furthermore, it removes chance encounters from the informational environment that would bring insight and learning. Personalization could prevent users from coming into contact with new information and ideas that can change the way they think about the world (Pariser, 2011). The circumstance that most users do not know that search results are personalized aggravates the filter bubble effect (Hannak, Sapiezynski, Molavi Kakhki, Krishnamurthy, Lazer, Mislove & Wilson, 2013). Personalized search holds the risk of unwanted and unrecognized manipulation. Furthermore, personalized search requires the collection of personal data and holds the risk of violation of privacy rights. For these reasons, personalized search is not considered any further in this work.

This work aims at a language-independent solution, because this allows to apply the approach to user-generated content independent of origin and language. The Web was meant to be an information system for the entire world and that is what it became (Berners-Lee, 1996, p. 69). Like the Web in general, user-generated content is a world wide matter. The advantages of language-independence are hence especially substantial: A language-independent approach allows to compare user-generated content worldwide. Moreover, the adaption of a language-dependent approach to other languages requires additional resources, which are spared in a language-independent approach. Language-dependent approaches usually exploit language specifics, which do not always have correspondents in other languages. It can then be difficult if not impossible to apply such an approach to other languages. If a language-dependent approach is transferable, this can be complex and costly. An effort that is less likely to be made if a language is spoken by fewer people or in parts of the developing world.

This work addresses the above described problem for content that is contributed to the World Wide Web by one author and is publicly available. Hence, this work does not aim at a solution that is also applicable to collaboratively created content. It does also not cover private communication that is transferred via the Internet.[1]

This work aims to contribute a solution that allows to compare user-generated content by different metadata. This work does not intend

---

[1]Chapter 2 elaborately delimits user-generated content and the concept *public* as subject matter of this work.

to evaluate the value of information provided by these metadata. It is assumed that metadata—such as the number of people who read, liked and recommended a contribution—provide valuable information for the user's orientation. This work shall contribute to transparency, overview and comparability of these measures to support users in their task of discovery and evaluation of user-generated content. It does not aim at investigating the correlation of these measures and an assumed objective quality of the content, determined for example by experts.[2]

Information scientists build systems designed to be used by others. Consequently, the way a system is designed potentially affects many people. This is a task that involves responsibility. The ranking approach for user-generated content developed in this work is also intended to be used by many users. There are decisions that have been made based on other considerations than what is technically possible, feasible and efficient. Analyzing user-generated content tends to be associated with concerns about user's privacy. It is not always technically impossible to exploit user data beyond the user's knowledge and approval. Striving for responsible system design, requirements and conditions are imposed as follows:

1. *The user's privacy needs to be respected.*
   If content is made publicly available, it is assumed that the author intended to present this contribution publicly. If content is made available for a specified audience, content should not be crawled, analyzed and presented to other users.

2. *If crawling is not desired, this is respected.*
   Providers of online platforms might disapprove of crawling techno-

---

[2]For example, a research question could also be, what kind of user-generated content users prefer. An imaginable result could be that well-written, long, informative essays are poorly rated by other users, whereas the comparison-rating of an expert group rates those contributions as excellent. Thus, it could be concluded that other users' ratings and quality do not correlate. But, it is not the intention of this work to evaluate the preferences of a group of experts against the preferences of Internet users.

logies that go through the content to store or analyze it. Whether crawling is desired can be declared in `robot.txt`. Every crawler that is used for the purpose of this work needs to parse a platform's `robot.txt` for approval before collecting data.

3. *The solution should aim at comprehensibility.*
   The aspired modeling for the ranking should be transparent and easy to understand for the user. It should not only deliver a good relevance ranking, but also allow the user to comprehend its elements. Background of this consideration is that an algorithm that is transparent to the user is less prone to manipulation. Additionally, the user should not have to comprehend the ranking to be able to use it.

The methodology applied to develop a solution to the problem comprises the following steps: First, a classification based on similarities among platforms is introduced. Then, available metadata is collected for representative platforms of each category. The collection of metadata is then analyzed for commonalities throughout platforms and platform-specific metadata. A model for metadata is introduced that comprises the structure all user-generated content units have in common. Based on this, a query-independent ranking approach is developed that allows to compare and rank user-generated content from all categories.

The subsequent chapters of this work are organized as follows:

In Chapter 2 fundamentals, including definitions and explanations of concepts related to the subject matter and already informally used in this chapter, such as user-generated content, social media, and publishing are introduced. The impact user-generated content has on the individual, society and economy are described. Furthermore, the challenges that accompany user-generated content and how users cope with them are discussed. Finally, weaknesses of existing approaches for the evaluation of user-generated content are addressed.

Chapter 3 provides a summary of the collection and analysis of metadata of user-generated content from all categories. Derived from the analysis, a structure for user-generated content units that applies to all categories is presented.

Information retrieval is the field of research in computer science that provides methods to solve problems concerning retrieval and ranking of documents, though not specifically for the application domain of user-generated content. Chapter 4 introduces concepts of information retrieval as means to solve the initial problem. Furthermore, difficulties that result from the specific application-domain of user-generated content are identified.

Chapter 5 presents a query-independent ranking approach for user-generated content that allows to compare and rank user-generated content units from different platforms.

In Chapter 6 a user-generated content discovery engine and a user-generated content search engine are presented as examples for applications of the developed approach.

Finally, Chapter 7 concludes with a summary of the most important results of this work and gives an outline of potentials for further work and research.

2 User-Generated Content

Realizing the value of social media
requires innovative computing research.
Shneiderman, Preece & Pirolli (2011, p. 34)

Social media, especially user-generated content, is a relatively young field of research. A research community is just forming around the topic. There is no common understanding of the subject, yet. Therefore, the following Chapter begins with an introduction of the notion of user-generated content and related terms for the work at hand in Section 2.1. I shall also give a summary of the range of understandings existing among other scientists. Furthermore, the classification of user-generated content is established that this work is based on.

User-generated content has effects on society, economy and the individual user himself. The fundamental changes and the potential that user-generated content is accompanied by are addressed in Section 2.2. But, the possibility for every user to publish content also causes a huge amount of information. The navigation through and classification of this information becomes a growing challenge for users. The user's possibilities to classify user-generated content today are presented in Section 2.3.

There are several works that aim at social media analysis or ranking. Some of them exploit every detail of information given for a specific kind of user-generated content allowing interesting computer-generated insights. The more an approach is specialized for a specific

platform, the more it tends to exploit platform specifics, which are
difficult to transfer to other platforms. The specialization causes a
lack of cross-platform comparability. Existing approaches and their
compatibility with other platforms are subject of Section 2.4.

2.1 What User-Generated Content Is and What It Is Not

There are several different terms that evolved around the subject of
user-generated content and the technology that enables its creation.
Web 2.0, social media, social Web, read/write Web, social comput-
ing, social software, collective action tools, socio-technical systems,
computer-mediated communication, consumer-generated media, user-
generated content, virtual communities, online communities are some
of them. For each term there is a variety of notions. In the following,
the terminology used in the work at hand is introduced. Additionally,
an overview of the variety of notions in related works is provided.

2.1.1 Terminology for Key Concepts Used in this Work

The democratization of information, the shift from one-to-many to
many-to-many communication, and the transformation from consuming to publishing users of the Internet are essential aspects of social
media (e.g., Lessig, 2001; Münker, 2009; Hansen, Shneiderman &
Smith, 2010; Solis, 2010; Anderson, 2012). The user's ability to make
content available to many people forms the basis of these aspects.
Making content available to a large group once required printing and
a publisher. Through social media it has become possible for almost[1]

---

[1]Of course, there are still basic requirements such as online access. It is important
to be aware of potential regional differences. Inequalities in terms of access
to information and communication technologies between countries or regions
are known as **digital divide**. The world share of internet users grew from
18 percent in 2006 to 35 percent in 2011. Still, regional differences remain.

everyone to make information publicly available without the need of a publisher.

According to the Encyclopædia Britannica (2007, p. 415), publishing is "the activity that involves the selection, preparation, and distribution of written and visual matter." Examples for published matter are books, magazines and newspapers. The traditional view of publishing regards only printed matters as published matters. But, since "electronic books and online newspapers" are also reckoned to be types of publishing, the printed form is no longer a requirement for publishing (Encyclopædia Britannica, 2007, p. 416). The Encyclopædia Britannica itself—after a history of almost 240 years of printed editions[2]—is no longer printed, but is exclusively accessible online.[3] Although, in many cases of digital publishing the principles of printed publishing still apply, it becomes difficult to mark the boundaries of publishing clearly. The technical progress has changed the traditional notion of publishing.

To apply the concept of publishing in the context of social media, it has to be rendered more precisely. In the context of this work, **to publish** means making information publicly available. To adapt the concept to social media, several levels of public are distinguished. **General public** means that no receiver is specified by the contributing user. The content is available for everyone. This means that the audience is potentially unlimited. **Limited public** means that no receiver is explicitly specified by the contributing user, but the audience is limited. The limitation can be caused by platforms that require registration prior to reading. This is the case, for example, if a platform presents its content only to registered users; although anyone might be admitted to register, the audience is limited to the re-

---

Average Internet penetration levels in developing regions rose to 26 percent by 2011. In sub-Saharan Africa however, they remain below 15 percent. (United Nations, 2012)

[2]The first edition of the Encyclopædia Britannica was issued in 1768 (Encyclopædia Britannica, 2007). The last printed version was published in 2007.

[3]http://www.britannica.com/

gistered users. Limited public can be subdivided into known-limited public and unknown-limited public. **Known-limited public** comprises the cases when no receiver is specified but the audience is limited to known people. An example is content shared with a group, such as *friends* in social networks.[4] This example illustrates that known-limited public is similar to private. **Unknown-limited public** describes the case when the audience is limited but not exclusively to known people. An example is when content is shared with a closed community such as *friends of friends* in social networks.

If the audience is limited to specified receivers, it is called **private**. In the context of this work, private communication is not user-generated content. This means, telephone calls, written letters, faxes, emails, SMS, instant messages, and so on, do not fall under the notion of user-generated content as it is used in this thesis. However, private communication can be part of a social media platform. Social networks for instance, usually allow to publish content to the general public, to a limited public as well as private messages.

In social media, the user who contributes a piece of content does not need to define his audience, but he can limit the audience. **Reach** is the number of people who receive a message. The less the audience is limited by a contributor, the more potential reach the message has. The degree of intimacy increases with limitation of the audience. Figure 2.1 shows the private and public levels of communication. Their characteristics are illustrated in relation to reach and intimacy.

This notion of *public*, adapted for user-generated content, replaces the concept of *sender and receiver* by *contributor and audience*. The **contributor** is the user who published a message. The contributor does not necessarily have to be the creator of the content. Whether or not the contributor is the creator of the content, in social media he is usually[5] displayed as *author* and will therefore be referred to as **author**.

---

[4]For more information about social networks refer to Subsection 2.1.3
[5]In some cases, platforms display citations.

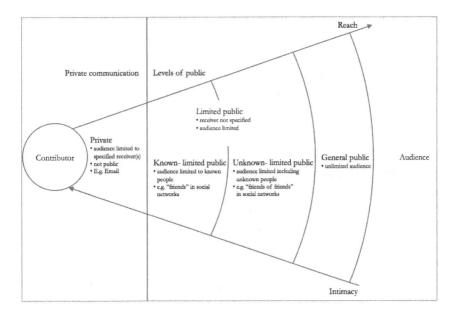

Figure 2.1: Reach-Intimacy-Model.
The Reach-Intimacy-Model illustrates private communication and the levels of public for user-generated content in relation to reach and intimacy. Private communication is not regarded as user-generated content.

In the context of this work, the central characteristic for user-generated content is the possibility for users to publish content to others.

User-generated content is content published on an online platform by users. The term **social media** comprises platforms that contain user-generated content. Users do not need programming skills to publish content on a social media platform.

Whether content contributed by a company on a social media platform is considered user-generated content, depends on the notion of *user*. *User* can refer to the *user of a social media platform*. In this case, the content contributed by a company on a social media platform would be regarded as user-generated content. *User* can also refer to *private individual* as opposed to *professional* or *business person*. In this case, the content contributed by a company on a social media platform would not be considered user-generated content. In the context of this work, **user** refers to the user of a social media platform.

For search engines the smallest unit is a Web page with a URL as identifier. For user-generated content this view does not sufficiently apply. One Web page, one URL usually contains several social media entries from different authors. For social media the smallest unit is the **user-generated content unit.** A user-generated content unit is one single contribution by one author at a given time. Collaboratively created content usually has more than one author. This case is not covered in this thesis.

A user-generated content unit consists of core data and metadata. The given piece of information—the content—is the **core data.** **Metadata** is information about a given piece of information (Baeza-Yates & Ribeiro-Neto, 2003). Examples for metadata about user-generated content are *date of publication, status of the author in the community*, and *number of views*.

In this work, opinions that are expressed by one click are also referred to as **one-click-opinions.** Examples are Facebook's *likes*, Google's *+1*, Youtube's *thumbs up*, and so on. Ratings of user-generated content units by other users are **peer-ratings.**

2.1.2 The Variety of Terminologies in Related Works

Aside from the notion of social media and user-generated content used in this work, there is a variety of other notions used in other authors' works. It is important to be aware of this whenever key terms are used without further explanation. There is no consensus about which platforms and services belong to social media and which do not.

Many works about social media do not explicitly address the question what is meant by *social media*. This implies that it is often assumed that there is a common understanding about what the term *social media* refers to. But, a closer look at the uses of the term reveals that there is actually a variety of notions.

One might suspect that because there is not a uniform conception, there are many descriptions in various publications about the topic. But as a matter of fact, attempts to define the terms are rare. To many it is not exactly clear what social media is and what it is not (Lovett, 2011). Many existing descriptions for social media are incomplete, imprecise, or contradicting. Anderson (2012, p. 1) speculates that the reasons for this shortcoming might be the relative novelty of the subject or the "slippery character" of the subject "that's hard to pin down."

This is also the case for related terms such as *Web 2.0* and *user-generated content*. Some authors use the terms synonymously to social media, whereas others make a difference between them. Grabs & Bannour (2011) for example, describe Web 2.0 as the possibility for every user to create content and to share them via different channels among each other. They do not differentiate between the terms *Web 2.0* and *user-generated content* and use them interchangeably. Another example is Münker's interpretation of Web 2.0, which is also very similar to what others describe as social media. He describes Web 2.0 as the trend to design a Web page in a way that it is considerably co-designed by its users. The degree of participation may vary from commenting or rating like it is practice at Amazon[6] to platforms where the content is exclusively created by users (Münker, 2009).

Others use the term *Web 2.0* to stress technical aspects, such as AJAX and open APIs, whereas *social Web* or *social media* are used to stress social aspects (e.g., Anderson, 2012; Lessig, 2001).

The term *Web 2.0* has been coined with a different meaning. It can be tracked back to Knorr (2003) quoting Dietzen who "calls the Web 2.0,

---

[6]http://www.amazon.com

where the Web becomes a universal, standards-based integration platform." It became popular when O'Reilly (2005) published an article titled "What is Web 2.0" about the ideas and changes behind the Web 2.0 concept.

Despite the expectations the title of the article might evoke, O'Reilly does not describe *the* Web 2.0 as form or enhancement of the World Wide Web. Instead he uses the term as an adjective and describes principles that he considers as the core competencies of companies that *are* Web 2.0. Examples are "companies that provide services with cost-effective scalability instead of packaged software are Web 2.0", "Web 2.0 companies trust users as co-developers", and "companies that are Web 2.0 have lightweight user interfaces, development models and business models" (O'Reilly, 2005). O'Reilly also provides "Web 2.0 Design Patterns" with recommendations for companies that want to become Web 2.0. These examples illustrate O'Reilly's business driven point of view when he uses the term *Web 2.0*.

Kaplan & Haenlein explicitly address the question of what social media is. Their attempt to define social media is often referenced (e.g., Fischer & Reuber, 2011; Foster, Francescucci & West, 2010; Nack, 2010; Wikipedia, 2013a,b). Kaplan & Haenlein agree that there seems to be confusion as to what should be included in the term *social media* and how it differs from *Web 2.0*. They dedicate a section to the question "What is Social Media—And what is not?" Herein, they characterize social media as "a group of Internet-based applications that build on the ideological and technological foundations of Web 2.0, and that allow the creation and exchange of User Generated Content." Meanwhile, Web 2.0 is described as "the platform for the evolution of Social Media" and "Web 2.0 represents the ideological and technological foundation." User-generated content is "the sum of all ways in which people make use of Social Media." (Kaplan & Haenlein, 2010, p. 60 ff)

Rephrasing their circular reference, the three terms are not synonymous, but related and are somehow a foundation for each other. Social media refers to applications, Web 2.0 refers to underlying technological aspects, whereas user-generated content is specified as "ways of use." It is a suggestion for how to arrange the concepts towards each other. But Kaplan and Heanlein do not offer a definition for what social media is and what it is not. They do not specify "people" in context of "user-generated content." Considering blogs, it remains unclear whether Kaplan & Haenlein would consider blogs published by professionals and journalists as "user-generated content." Companies use microblogs such as Twitter and social networks such as Facebook for communication, too. It is unspecified whether they regard this kind of content "user-generated content."

There are also inconsistent uses of terms and very broad conceptions that describe much more than online communication and user participation. Safko (2010, p. 3) claims: "Social media is the media we use to be social. That's it." This would also include telephones, emails, letters and so on, none of which are addressed in his book. Hansen et al. (2010, p. 12) see social media as "a set of online tools that supports social interaction between users. The term is often used to contrast with more traditional media such as television and books that deliver content to mass populations but do not facilitate the creation or sharing of content by users." But then they include also corporate Web sites (e.g., www.ford.com) in their taxonomy of social media, which—as television and books—only deliver content and do not facilitate the creation or sharing of content by users (Hansen et al., 2010).

Summing up, there is no terminology that is universally agreed upon. A variety of other notions is used in other authors' works. Recent works which broach the issue of terminology show no clear tendency that the different understandings are converging towards a consensus. Consequently, it is important to pay attention to the specific notions that underlie key terms in other works.

2.1.3 Social Media Categories Used in this Work

Resulting from the divergent comprehension there is a series of different opinions about which platforms belong to social media and how they can be categorized. Most works contain enumerations of platforms with an exemplary character instead of methodically built taxonomies. Whenever social media categories are mentioned without further elaboration, there is a range of interpretations.

There are numerous platforms that allow users to publish content and belong to social media. Constantly more are emerging. A proper categorization should include all platforms that meet the underlying definition of social media. Categories should be methodically derived from a feasible criterion.

In the context of this work, platforms are allocated to categories by the type of metadata provided by the platforms.[7] This way to categorize social media platforms is chosen because it is especially suited for query-independent ranking of user-generated content that utilizes metadata to evaluate content units.

The following classification will serve as basis of understanding for this work:

1. Blogs

2. Forums

3. Location sharing and annotation platforms

4. Media sharing platforms

5. Microblogs

6. Question and answer platforms

7. Rating and review platforms

8. Social networks

---

[7]For the detailed analysis of metadata of user-generated content from different platforms refer to Chapter 3.

The following provides a short characterization for each category. The sets of characteristics of categories are not necessarily disjoint. Some platforms allocated in a certain category can have aspects of other categories. For example, social networks allow to share pictures and videos as it is typical for media sharing platforms.

Blogs are a special form of Web sites keeping publication deceptively simple. Entries are displayed in reverse chronological order, presenting the most recent entry at the top of the page. The term blog is a short form of Weblog, a neologism derived from the combination of the terms *World Wide Web* and *log* as in logbook. Jon Barger coined the term *Weblog* in 1997 (Ammann, 2009). Shortly after, the term blog was used as noun and verb likewise. The first Weblogs were public online diaries. Blogs can be differentiated by the number of users authorized to publish blog entries into single- and multi-authored blogs.[8] Until the mid 2000s blogs were usually written by one author. In recent years multi-author blogs have become popular as well (Safko, 2010). Bloggers tend to evolve their blogs around a special interest (Macdonald, Santos, Ounis & Soboroff, 2010). Blogs can also be distinguished by the degree of professionalism of the content produced into professional- and private-content blogs. Blogs range from personal diaries to professional journalists' and corporate blogs.

A **forum** is an online discussion site where people can hold conversations in form of posted messages. Conversations are organized in **threads** and are stored permanently. A thread belongs to a topic. It consists of a root-posting and replies. In open forums content is public and can be read by everyone. In closed forums it is necessary to become a member of the forum-community to read the postings. To actively take part in a discussion it is usually necessary to become a member. Forums have a hierarchic structure. Figure 2.2 illustrates the different hierarchy levels of forums. The first level displays a list of topics that are covered by the forum. Threads covering the same topic are collected in a sub-forum. Threads are on a lower level. They

---

[8]Note that also in multi-authored blogs content units are usually not collaboratively contributed.

start with a root-posting containing a question, topic or statement. A thread consists of one or more postings, which are organized by the time of submission, usually in chronological order. Some forums offer their members the possibility to connect with each other, as it is common in social networks. But unlike in social networks, users can read discussions and contributions whether or not they are connected. Members can discuss topics with any other member, being connected is not a precondition. Hence, the average forum user has fewer connections than the average social network user. Forums exist since the early days of the Internet and they form rich repositories of collaborative knowledge (Wanas, El-Saban, Ashour & Ammar, 2008).

Location sharing and annotation platforms apply location based services that enable groups of friends to share their current location and annotations. Location based services allow people to see where they are geographically with the help of GPS equipped mobile phones. Examples are applications that help the user to navigate from A to B, locating others on a map displayed on the phone or receiving information about traffic jam ahead (Rogers, Sharp & Preece, 2011). Examples for location sharing and annotation platforms are Foursquare,[9] Loopt,[10] Facebook Places,[11] and Google Latitude.[12] They allow users to plot their location and share it with other users (Cramer, Rost & Holmquist, 2011). Users can also create places, upload pictures, videos and leave written messages for others.

Media sharing refers to platforms where registered users can upload their content and share it with friends or provide it to the public (e.g., Flickr,[13] Youtube[14]). Other users can rate and comment on the content.

---

[9]https://de.foursquare.com
[10]http://www.loopt.com
[11]https://www.facebook.com/about/location
[12]http://www.google.com/latitude
[13]http://www.flickr.com
[14]http://www.youtube.com

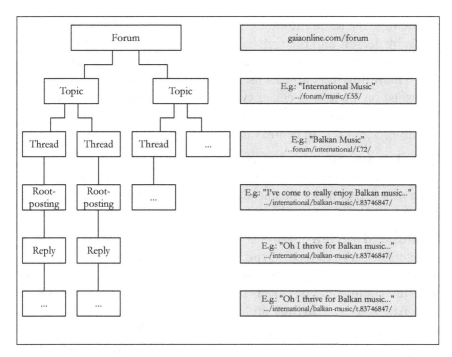

Figure 2.2: Hierarchical structure of forums.
Forums first provide a list of topics. When a user clicks on a topic he navigates to a list of threads. Threads consist of a root-posting and a list of replies.

Microblogs allow users to share information by broadcasting short, real-time messages. A well-known microblog provider is Twitter.[15] People share opinions, daily life activities, news, and so on with friends, families, co-workers, as well as strangers (Grace, Zhao & Boyd, 2010). Microblogs differ from traditional blogs. Content units are limited in size. A Twitter post for example is limited to 140 characters. A microblog entry consists of a short text or a link to images or videos. Due to its size limits, microblogging posts are less dialogue oriented and often focused on one issue (Zhao & Rosson, 2009). Using

---

[15]http://www.twitter.com

microblogs, the author does not specify a recipient. Every message is public by default and the recipients choose whose messages they read, whom they **follow**. Users who follow someone are called her **followers**. The **followings** are the users whom she follows. A content unit published on Twitter is called **tweet**. A *tweet* cited by someone else is called a **retweet**. Category assignments or tags are marked with a number sign (#). In context of Twitter those are called **hashtags**.

Question and answer platforms are platforms where users can pose questions and everyone can answer them. Answers can be rated by other users. Examples for question and answer platforms are Yahoo! Answers,[16] Gutefrage.net,[17] Ask,[18] and Blurtit.[19]

Rating and review platforms allow users to rate and comment on products or services (e.g., Qype,[20] Ciao,[21] Tripadvisor[22]). There are rating and review platforms that are completely user-generated and there are commercial platforms that integrate user-generated content (e.g., Amazon[23]). **Ratings** are opinions that can be contributed by just one click on a given scale. The scale can be binary (e.g., *thumbs up*), or it can have more levels (e.g., *x out of n stars*). **Reviews** are written texts about products, services or experiences. Usually, platforms allow both, ratings and reviews.

Social networks are platforms that allow individuals to create a profile and articulate a list of other users with whom they share a connection. Users can view and traverse their connections (Boyd & Ellison, 2008). Examples for social networks are Myspace,[24] Face-

---

[16] http://answers.yahoo.com
[17] http://www.gutefrage.net
[18] http://ask.com
[19] http://www.blurtit.com
[20] http://www.qype.com
[21] http://www.ciao.com
[22] http://www.tripadvisor.com
[23] http://www.amazon.com
[24] http://www.myspace.com

book,[25] LinkedIn,[26] Google+,[27] and Xing.[28] Social networks support **feeds** consisting of updates, which are similar to mircoblog posts. The circle of people updates are published to, differs gradually from public to personal. In some social networks, relationships are mutual relations, in others they can be unidirectional as it is in Google+. The social network Facebook has 1.15 billion monthly active users as of June 2013 (Facebook, 2013).

2.2 The Value of User-Generated Content

The possibility to make content publicly available is a major achievement in human history that enables intellectual development and progress. The possibility for everyone to contribute content to the public is accompanied by new chances as well as challenges. To grasp the full potential of social media, values as well as challenges need to be understood.

2.2.1 A Short History of Publication

Before the invention of writing, information could be spread by word-of-mouth only, with all the accompanying limitations. Publication began after the monopoly of letters, mostly held by a priestly caste, had been broken. Scripts of various kinds came to use, but book production was confined largely by religious centers of learning. The invention of printing transformed the possibilities of the written word. Printing has been first invented in China in the 6th century A.D., but it was not passed on to Europe. In Europe the invention of printing is attributed to Gutenberg about 1440–1450. His achievements involved movable metal type, paper, ink, and press. In less than 50 years print-

---

[25]http://www.facebook.com
[26]http://www.linkedin.com
[27]https://plus.google.com
[28]http://www.xing.com

ing was carried out from Germany to Europe. The possibilities for mass-producing written matter soon became evident. Additionally, around the turn of the century literacy began to spread beyond the clergy. Every kind of attempt was made to regulate such a "dangerous" new mode of communication (Encyclopædia Britannica, 2007, p. 416). After three centuries of struggle around freedom of the press, by the end of the 18th century a large measure of freedom of press has been achieved in western Europe and in North America and a wide range of printed matter was in circulation. The mechanization of printing and increasing literacy brought the printed word to its powerful position as means of influencing people and, hence, societies. By the 19th century, publishing became a distinct occupation. Selecting, editing, designing the material, arranging its production and distribution and bearing the financial risk became functions peculiar to a publisher. (Encyclopædia Britannica, 2007)

In the early 20th century the technical requirements for electronic dissemination of audio and video information were developed. At the beginning of the 20th century radio and in the middle of the 20th century television became important media to broadcast information. (Encyclopædia Britannica, 2013a)

The development of the World Wide Web began in 1989. Tim Berners-Lee and his colleagues at CERN created the HyperText Transfer Protocol and released the first Web browser in 1992. By the mid-1990s the World Wide Web had millions of active users (Encyclopædia Britannica, 2013c). With the World Wide Web it became possible to spread information via the Internet. Making information publicly available was no longer a monopoly of printing. To publish content via the Internet instead of a publisher a specialist was needed who had the technical knowledge how to make the content available online.

The first form of social media emerged with the creation of the USENET in 1979 (Encyclopædia Britannica, 2013b). The USENET, in full User's Network, is an Internet-based network of discussion groups. In the 2000s social media emerged as a significant phenomenon. It transforms the possibilities of communication. To spread information, neither a publisher nor a specialist is needed anymore. Information can be spread by everyone. The amount of information publicly available has increased drastically. This goes hand in hand with the progress of mobile devices that are equipped with photo and video capabilities while providing mobile access to the Internet.

The number of people who are able to publish content has increased. The possibilities to publish have been simplified. And the creation of content has been facilitated as well. Since a publisher is no longer needed to make content publicly available, the selection of content falls to the user. The publisher's filtering of the content with regards to quality is omitted. Consequently, there is a huge amount of information. It is the user's task now to select and evaluate it. This is a new challenge for users, which requires new competences and means.

2.2.2 Social Media Becomes a News Source

Content created and contributed by users can be of high value. Due to smart phones[29] and the number of users contributing content, news can spread faster around the world than through any other media. In January 2009 US Airways flight 1549 made an emergency landing on the Hudson River. It was an accident in a metropolitan area during daylight hours. The news about the accident were spread by eyewitnesses via social media. The first Twitter message about the plane crash came from Hanrahan (2009) a few minutes after the plane went down: "I just watched a plane crash into the hudson rive in manhattan." Figure 2.3 shows a picture of the plane taken with a mobile phone camera and made publicly available via Twitter.

---

[29]The key features of smart phones relevant here are mobile Internet access, photo and video camera.

There's a plane in the Hudson. I'm on the ferry going to pick up the people. Crazy.   👁 904,087   1669 days ago

Figure 2.3: Picture of US Airways flight 1549 taken with a mobile device and shared on Twitter.

Krums (2009) took this picture of the US Airways plane that ditched on the Hudson River 15 January, 2009 and shared it via Twitter shortly after the plane came down.

The first report about the event on television was aired 30 minutes after the crash by CNN (2009). This example illustrates that via social media information can be spread faster than via newspapers, television or radio.

2.2.3 Social Media Empowers Civil Movements

In social media there is no central institution that selects the events that become news. The users who view and share information on social media platforms decide whether an event is breaking news. News agencies and editorial departments decide what is delivered as news in television, radio and newspapers. This selection influences the recipients' view of the world. In countries where there are restraints upon freedom of speech and of the press, filtering of information by the government is an instrument to manipulate its citizens. Social media plays a decisive role in democracy movements in countries with censored press and a lack of freedom of speech.

The Arab Spring was a wave of protests against authoritarian regimes in the Middle East and North Africa in 2010 and 2011. In all Arab countries the press was under censorship.[30] Some journalists paid with their lives for their views (Khazen, 1999). Social media played an essential role in the Arab Spring.

In Tunisia, the first protests were catalyzed when Mohamed Bouazizi—a 26-year-old street vendor—immolated himself on December 17, 2010 in Sidi Bouzid, protesting his treatment by local officials. The terrestrial TV stations were strictly state controlled and did not report on the events in Sidi Bouzid. A video was taken by eyewitnesses who were filming with their mobile phones. One of them subsequently uploaded the material of the self-immolation to his public Facebook account. Through Facebook the material was accessible to Al Jazeera, the Qatar-based satellite TV station, which

---

[30]This included Egypt, Algeria, Saudi Arabia, Sudan, Bahrain, Qatar, Tunisia (Khazen, 1999).

broadcast the news on this event via Satellite TV. In the course of the evolving uprising, citizens on-site continued to take photos and videos of the demonstrations with mobile phones and uploaded them to the Internet. Through Facebook a significant amount of activists informed people outside Sidi Bouzid about what was happening in the town. These country-wide social networks spread the news about the ongoing political activities in Sidi Bouzid to other cities in Tunisia. In other Tunisian cities (e.g., Reguets, Kasserine, Taba, and Sfax) demonstrations followed soon. The organizers of local demonstrations used Facebook to develop and communicate their strategies, such as where to gather or where to build barricades overnight. The first demonstration with a nationwide call for participation in Tunis was organized mainly via Facebook (Wulf, Misaki, Atam, Randall & Rohde, 2013).

Egypt was governed by the authoritarian regime of Hosni Mubarak from 1981 to 2011. During this time emergency law was in effect. The emergency law allowed prosecutors to detain any citizen for up to 30 days without charges (Moustafa, 2003). Egyptians suffered poverty, corruption and political repression. In the Egyptian revolution social media also played a key role for pro-democracy protesters (Preston, 2011). In June 2010, Khaled Said—a young Egyptian—was pulled from an Internet cafe in Alexandria by the police. He was then beaten to death by the police in the lobby of a residential building. The Egyptian Ghonim (2012) created a Facebook page "We Are All Khaled Said". Pictures taken with a mobile phone from the morgue of Said's battered and bloodied face were posted there. Within a week 130,000 people joined the page and shared updates about the case. The Facebook page was used to post invitations to street protests and silent protests in Alexandria and Cairo. Video-enabled cell phones shed light on the injustices and cruelties of the government's practices that would have happened in the dark without public notice otherwise. The Facebook page provided a possibility for people to connect with each other. It offered Egyptians a forum to bond over their outrage about the government's abuses. The Facebook page

"We Are All Khaled Said" helped to ignite the uprising that led to the protests that forced President Hosni Mubarak from power in 2011 (Vargas, 2012).

Cases of human-rights violations exposed and made public by citizens are reported from many countries. There are videos on Youtube calling attention to cotton-growers' working conditions in Uzbekistan, mining practices in the Philippines, human-organ harvesting in China, the persecution of Bahai's in Iran and Malaysian police practices and many more crimes against humanity (Diamond, 2010).

2.2.4 Social Media Facilitates Ethical Consumerism

Also in democratically reigned countries there are grievances that do not have a lobby among traditional media (i.e., print, television and radio) authorities, but which do concern people as citizens and also as consumers.

Social media enables people to disseminate information about such issues. Examples for areas of concern are nature protection and animal welfare (e.g., environmental reporting, nuclear power, climate change, pollution, animal testing, factory farming), economic issues (e.g., supply chain policy, marketing, product sustainability), and political issues such as armaments and anti-social finance. Consumers' attempts to persuade companies to sustainable and responsible behavior with the help of their collective consuming behavior is called **ethical consumerism**.

An example from Kenya illustrates the impact of ethical consumerism. In Kenya, women working conditions in the cut flower industry improved with the country's success in supplying European markets (Hale & Opondo, 2005). When Kenya started to supply European markets, it brought increased attention to the industry's social and environmental impacts. Driven by the various concerns of consumers, retailers, auctions, European regulators and civil society organizations, flower growers have to comply with a number of codes of conduct. Due to these codes Kenya's cut flower industry evolved as one of the most codified agricultural sectors in the world (Opondo, 2013). Codes of conduct were initially introduced to satisfy consumers and retailers in the European markets, but they have led to a noteworthy improvement of working conditions on the flower farms and packhouses (Opondo, 2013).

Consumers' boycotts of products and companies due to ethical reasons have a long history (Irving, Harrison & Rayner, 2002). The positive counterpart is called buycott or carrotmob (Neilson, 2010). Consumers share their knowledge about responsible businesses and purchase their goods in order to reward socially responsible behavior (Hoffmann & Hutter, 2012). With the help of social media ethical consumerism can gain impact. It facilitates the exposition and distribution of malpractice as well as responsible behavior and helps consumers to organize and coordinate boycotts as well as buycotts.

2.2.5 Social Media Supports Word-of-Mouth

Information about products or services provided by the producer or retailer of the product is biased due to the producer's or retailer's interest to sell it. Information provided by consumers for consumers is called **word-of-mouth**. For consumers, word-of-mouth is an alternative source of information about products. Product information provided by other consumers who are free of commercial interests are considered to be less biased and hence more truthful. They are considered to be a valuable source of information for users in their decision making process (Lelis & Howes, 2011).

User-generated content by consumers about products or services are the online version of traditional word-of-mouth. Users share their product experiences and opinions with others on social media platforms. Product experiences and opinions can be found in all types of social media platforms, such as blogs, forums and social networks, but rating and review platforms are especially dedicated to this purpose.

They help customers find products matching their needs (Chen & Xie, 2008). Studies show that user recommendations from social media influence purchase decisions (Reichelt, 2013). In some circumstances consumer trust online word-of-mouth sources even more than information from people known in person (Pöyry, Parvinen, Salo, Blakaj & Tiainen, 2011).

Although ratings and reviews can be a valuable source of unbiased information, there are also companies, which try to counterfeit social media recommendations. Users are sensitive to such manipulations. In 2010 the CEO of the company WeTab Helmut Hoffer von Ankershoffen pretended to be a consumer and wrote very positive product reviews about his own company's product as "Peter Glaser" on Amazon. The fake was revealed and followed by an outrage of potential customers. Figure 2.4 shows screen-shots of the review and the user's profile revealing that the author of the reviews actually is the CEO of the producing company. Helmut Hoffer von Ankershoffen resigned due to this scandal (DPA, 2010).

Thus, the manipulation of customer reviews is not trivial and can have serious consequences. Nevertheless, there are counterfeit reviews. Not all of them can be revealed at first sight. Some can only be detected by experienced users, others not at all. Online word-of-mouth is generated in unprecedented volume and at great speed (Zhang, Guo & Goes, 2013). Among several negative reviews a false positive review is often suspicious but carries no significant weight.

The possibility to share information about products and services with other users on rating and review platforms enlarges the circle of people experiences can be shared with. Formerly, people shared their experiences with people known in person. Nowadays, experiences can be shared online with everyone who is interested. Consequently, positive as well as negative information about products and services can spread faster and wider. Online word-of-mouth is an additional source of information that makes users independent from producers' or retailers' information about their products and services.

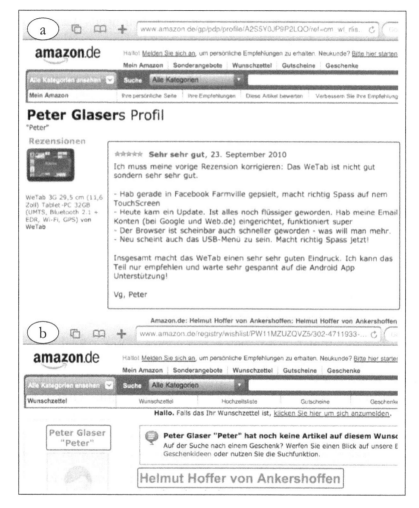

Figure 2.4: Example of a failed attempt to counterfeit a user recommendation.
a: WeTab CEO Helmut Hoffer von Ankershoffen wrote positive product reviews on his own product pretending to be Peter Glaser.
b: His Amazon wish list showed his true identity and revealed the deceit. Screen-shots from Spiegel (2010).

2.2.6 Social Media Extends Market Research

Experiences and opinions published by customers are also of value for market research. Analyzing user opinions in social media to understand customers is the core goal of Social Media Monitoring. Social Media Monitoring analyses user-generated content over a given time period with regard to relevant marketing information, such as brand image, trends, customer preferences, or sentiments. Results can help to improve product design and customer support as well as campaign development and public relation activities.

There are several companies on the market that offer Social Media Monitoring. Examples are Attensity,[31] BIG,[32] Visible,[33] Nielsen,[34] and Radian6.[35] Capabilities of these companies are diverse. Usually, the content is analyzed with basic text mining technologies. Results are combined with statistics from collected metadata. Metadata used for this purpose is limited to the information provided over all social media categories; such are source, date of contribution and the nickname of the author. Typical statistics are the number of mentions of predefined keywords such as brand names.[36] It can be further analyzed by time, source and authors. Further information, such as peer ratings, how long the author has been part of the community, or how often the contribution has been read is usually either manually analyzed or not taken into account.

2.2.7 Intentions Determine the Value of Social Media

The possibility for users to publish content to other users without the barriers publishing in print once had, has great impact on the

---

[31] http://www.attensity.com
[32] http://www.big-social-media.com
[33] http://www.visibletechnologies.com/
[34] http://nmincite.com/
[35] http://www.salesforcemarketingcloud.com
[36] This is commonly referred to as *Share of Voice*.

individual, on society and economy. The values of social media are manifold. Social media becomes an alternative source for independent and unfiltered news. It empowers people to expose wrongdoing, report news, express resentment and mobilize protest against grievances. Social media enables committed consumers to broadcast information about responsible businesses and disseminate information about irresponsible behavior to adapt their consumption according to their ethical beliefs. Online word-of-mouth has become an alternative source of information for products and services and makes the consumer more independent of potentially false marketing promises.

Social media can expand political, social and economic freedom (Diamond, 2010). Of course, the power of social media can also be exploited and misused. The positive effects illustrated in the previous sections presupposes good intentions. Social media provides the possibility to spread the word and organize to do good, but—as any other media—it can also be utilized for the opposite. And, even if intentions are noble, people who are not well-informed or manipulated by wrong or misleading information can do harm despite of good intentions.

2.3 Users' Strategies to Interpret Metadata Today

100 hours of video are uploaded to Youtube every minute and 6 billion hours of video are watched each month on YouTube (Youtube, 2013). In 2011, Flickr—a media sharing platform for photos—announced the 6 billionth photo uploaded to their platform (Kremerskothen, 2011). The microblogging platform Twitter has over 200 million active users creating over 400 million Tweets each day (Wickre, 2013). The blog platform Tumblr[37] hosts 132.2 million blogs with 58.4 billion entries (Tumblr, 2013a).

---

[37]http://www.tumblr.com

To tap the full potential of social media, values as well as challenges need to be understood. The massive amount of information contributed is one of the biggest challenges for the user.

The main challenge posed by user-generated content is that the distribution of quality has high variance (Agichtein et al., 2008). The quality varies from excellent to worthless and abusive.

Users are confronted with the challenge to find, evaluate and classify content. Additional information can help the user to cope with this challenge. User-generated content is accompanied by various and differing information about its content.

For example, a *tweet* is accompanied by information about when it has been contributed, how many people have already shared the tweet, how many people liked the tweet and who contributed it. A forum entry shows when it has been contributed and the nickname of the contributor. With several navigational steps, the user can learn how many other entries have been created in a discussion, how many times a discussion has been viewed and how many active members belong to a forum's community.

To the user the metadata is initially a number she needs to interpret. Let us assume, a user tries to decide, whether a specific video she found on Youtube is popular. The video displays a number of 100 views. The question, whether a video is popular, can be answered in comparison to other videos' number of views. Hence, knowledge about the range of numbers of views for other videos makes the information about how many times a specific video has been viewed more valuable. To gain this knowledge, the user has to manually search for other numbers to compare with. An experienced user may have already seen a lot of other videos. She might have gained a feeling for how many views are a few, average, or a lot. But if she did not keep record of how many times other videos have been watched, her judgment can not be more than a gut feeling. And even if—hypothetically—she kept record of the number of views of the videos she has already watched; it would still not be representative. Furthermore, not all information that might help to evaluate the value of a contribution can be assessed on the same page where the content is displayed. Some information can be found on authors' profiles, some by following other links provided. For some information the user even has to navigate back to other sites. It requires the knowledge where the information is displayed to be able to acquire it. To get the number of views of a discussion in a forum for example, the user has to navigate to a higher level in the hierarchy of the forum.

This mechanism applies to virtually all metadata provided for user-generated content. Users cope with answering questions, such as: *Is a four out of five stars very good or just average for a hotel review? Is 15 likes a positive indication for the piece of content? Do twenty check-ins indicate a recommendable restaurant?*

Another possibility to filter user-generated content is via social connections. That is, users browse through user-generated content that has been selected and shared by their social circles. Social circles exist in social media platforms which allow users to create a profile and connect with other users they know. Users receive those messages that have been shared by the people they are connected with. Social networks are an example. But there are other social media platforms that allow to connect with other people as well. Microblogging services also work that way. Users decide whom they *follow*. The feeds displayed to a user by Twitter are determined by the *followed* users. Messages are distributed via people who are connected. This mechanism can be described as **social filtering**. Messages are filtered by the social connections the user has established.

Social filtering has advantages as well as disadvantages. It is effective in reducing the amount of information. But, a message is only delivered to a user if and only if his connections have received the message and shared it. This means, the user can only hope that "If the news is that important, it will find me."[38] (Stelter, 2008). There

---

[38]The New York Times dedicated an article to the question how young people find political news online. Originally, the quote is from a college student

is no possibility to perform a dedicated search for generally well distributed messages. The kind of messages a user receives and how fast it reaches him, depends on the quality and amount of his social connections. A user who is not well connected is more likely to miss out on well distributed messages than a user who is well connected. The influence the user has on this is limited and depends on his ability to connect with others. Users, who do not have many friends in social networks, such as Facebook, users, who don't know who to follow on Twitter or on Google+ are excluded from the information flow. They can not profit from social filtering.

Furthermore, some platforms have their own rankings. Facebook for example, ranks the content displayed on the user-specific feeds based on the user's individual connections to other users. Although the ranking is not completely transparent to the user, Facebook engineers Sanghvi & Steinberg gave some insights about the Facebook News Feed Algorithm at a Facebook developer conference. The Facebook query-independent feed rank is called EdgeRank: $\sum_{edges\ e} u_e * w_e * d_e$. Here, u_e is the affinity score between viewing user and edge creator, w_e is a weight for the edge type (e.g., create, comment, like, tag) and d_e is the time decay factor based on how long ago the edge was created. The affinity score resembles the relation between a viewing user and the item's creator. It is higher if the bound between the two is tighter. The bounds become tighter when messages are exchanged or the viewer visits the creator's Facebook profile often. Edge types are given a weight. A comment is considered more important than a *like*. Hence, it gets a higher weight. The time decay takes the assumption into account that the older an edge, the less important it becomes. These factors are multiplied for each edge. All edge scores of a contribution are added up to its EdgeRank. Only first degree edges are used in this algorithm. The EdgeRank is based on the relations between users, other users' reactions to the entry and recency.

---

who described the way she receives news online in a research focus group. It illustrates an attitude towards searching of a person who is used to and influenced by the use of social filtering.

Consequently, each content unit is ranked differently depending on the viewing user. Furthermore, it only ranks content shared with already established social connections on the specific platform.

To summarize, metadata helps users to evaluate content. It gradually becomes more helpful with more knowledge about the range and distribution of their values. The user has to acquire this knowledge through manual research. There is no tool that assists the user with this challenge so far. To tap the full potential of social media, values as well as challenges need to be understood and possibilities to cope with the challenges have to be developed. This work aims at supporting users with the task of evaluation of user-generated contents and the interpretation of its metadata.

2.4 Existing Approaches Lack Cross-Platform Compatibility

The following section explains the advantages and challenges of a ranking approach for user-generated content that is compatible with different social media platforms. Furthermore, existing query-independent ranking approaches for user-generated content are presented and their applicability to user-generated content from different platforms is discussed.

Cross-platform compatibility has several advantages. A ranking approach is cross-platform compatible, if the ranking approach is applicable to content units from different platforms. An advantage of a cross-platform compatible ranking approach is that two content units are comparable by their ranking. If content units are comparable by ranking, an order can be established across content units from different platforms.

This allows to apply the approach to a search engine that delivers content from more than one platform. A ranking approach which is limited to a specific platform would only be applicable in a search engine that delivers content from the platform the ranking has been designed for.

Furthermore, a platform-specific approach would only allow to compare results from user-generated content units from the same platform.

A cross-platform compatible approach on the contrary, does not limit the user to findings such as "the best scoring (e.g., most popular) video from Youtube" and "the best scoring (e.g., most popular) video from Vimeo."[39] With a cross-platform compatible approach it is possible to determine which is the best scoring content unit independent of its origin.

Furthermore, an approach that is applicable to different platforms and not dependent on platform specifics is more likely to be applicable to changes in the platform specifics and even to new platforms.

Query-dependent ranking approaches rank documents by their texts' correspondence with the query. Query-dependent ranking approaches are therefore per se compatible with different platforms as long as the ranked documents contain text.

Query-independent ranking approaches however exploit other characteristics of the ranked objects. A query-independent ranking approach for user-generated content that is cross-platform compatible is therefore accompanied by challenges. The characteristics that are most valuable for the evaluation of user-generated content—its metadata—varies with different platforms.

Existing ranking approaches can be divided into approaches that are compatible with different platforms but are query-dependent and approaches that are query-independent but platform-specific.

Platform-specific approaches rank user-generated content based on the features specific to a social media category. Those approaches are

---

[39]Vimeo (`https://vimeo.com/`) is a media sharing platform for videos, similar to Youtube.

not applicable to platforms that lack those specific features. Wanas
et al. for example, developed a ranking specifically for forums. A
peculiarity of forums is their hierarchical structure. Information is
distributed among several hierarchical levels. In forums within a
thread, postings often relate to each other giving the whole thread
a discussion-like character. These characteristics raise some specific
questions, such as how to handle hierarchical information, or how
the content should be analyzed. A thread could be analyzed per
content unit neglecting the context. Alternatively, analysis could be
thread-wise. This alternative raises the question of how to handle
content unit related metadata. Wanas et al. address these questions and propose a set of features specifically to analyze forums.
The feature set is based on a forum's hierarchical structure. They
introduce "OnSubForumTopic" and "OnThreadForumTopic." "On-
SubForumTopic" refers to the degree a post has remained relevant to
the sub-forum it resides in. This is done by creating a bag of words
from the combination of all the words in the sub-forum and then comparing the most frequent 10 percent of them to the words occurring
in each post's body and title. Given that the first posting of a thread
and its title determine the topic of a thread, "OnThreadTopic" describes the relevance of a post to the discussion it occurs in. This is
done analogically to "OnSubForumTopic" by comparing each posting's bag of words to the bag of words of the leading post. (Wanas
et al., 2008)

Moturu proposes an approach to quantify trustworthiness of social
media content. The research is focused on shared health using content from Wikipedia and Daily Strength. The forum Moturu analyses
allows members to connect with each other as *friends*. This is not
a common feature for forums. In contrast to social networks, getting connected is not necessary to discuss topics with other members.
Hence, the average user has fewer connections than the average social
network member does. Moturu proposes author social connectedness
as a feature to quantify trustworthiness. Social connectedness is expressed by the average number of friends for each friend the author

is connected with. This feature can only be applied to social media platforms that allow its users to connect with each other. (Moturu, 2010)

The average number of answers with references is a significant feature for quality of the question in question and answer platforms (Agichtein et al., 2008). This is only applicable to question and answer platforms, but not other kind of social media platforms. Blogs for example lack the question and answers structure.

Although there is no query-independent ranking approach that is applicable to all kinds of social media platforms, there are features that are transferable to other platforms. Features gained by text analysis are applicable to all user-generated content units that contain text.

Text length is an example for a commonly used feature (e.g., Moturu, 2010; Wanas et al., 2008). Text length, measured by word count, is available for every text and easy to determine. But interpretations differ. Wanas et al. (2008) give credit to postings that are close to the average posting length of the forum, whereas other works give credit to longer texts. The intention in rewarding average length is to value contributions that conform to the length of postings the community accepts as normal. It has to be questioned, whether the average length of a posting indeed reflects the posting length the community accepts as normal. Usually, in a forum every posting contributed is published, whether it is accepted by the community or not. A major part of the forum's contributions could consist of contributions that are considered as "too short" or "too long." These would still be posted. There is no community acceptance filter. Consequently, the average length of a posting is independent of the length of postings the community accepts. Works that give credit to longer texts, assume that the longer a contributions is, the more earnestness can be insinuated (e.g., Moturu, 2010; Hu, Lim, Sun, Lauw & Vuong, 2007).

Links within the text of a user-generated content unit can help to ascertain the source of information and indicate utility as they point to additional sources of information that can help the user (Moturu, 2010; Elgersma & de Rijke, 2008).

Agichtein et al. (2008) introduce a classification framework to automatically identify high-quality social media content for question and answer platforms. The task of identifying high-quality content is handled as binary classification problem. Their goal is to separate high-quality content from the rest. Questions and answers are analyzed separately. The results were measured against a quality categorization done by humans.

Agichtein et al. take user relationships and metadata into account. In question and answer platforms users actively participate in the regulation of the system by rating interesting questions and voting for good answers. They tested different features for their performance in indicating high quality content. They used indicators from punctuation and typos (ignorance of capitalization, particularly repeated ellipsis and question marks, irregular spacing, misspellings, out-of-vocabulary words), syntactic and semantic complexity (average number of syllables per word, readability measures), and grammaticality (e.g., part-of-speech tagging and categorizing syntactic patterns as more or less correct,[40] the distance between its language model and a given language model) as text derived features (Agichtein et al., 2008, p. 186). Those text derived features could be applied to other texts as well. The resulting values for precision and recall reveal that direct and indirect peer-ratings as well as text length are among the most significant features (Agichtein et al., 2008). In the case of the evaluated question and answer platform direct peer-ratings are number of stars, number of thumbs up and number of best answer. The number of clicks on the question thread, normalized by the average number of clicks for all questions in its category is an example for indirect ratings.

---

[40]The sequence "when—how—why to (verb)" as in "how to identify..." is typical for lower-quality questions, whereas the sequence "when—how—why (verb) (personal pronoun) (verb)" as in "how do I remove..." is more typical for correctly-formed content.

These examples of research that address automated analysis of user-generated content shall illustrate that existing research for automated rating and ranking of user-generated content focuses on platform-specific approaches.

Nevertheless, this research contributes insights for the interpretation of the applied metrics and their interpretations as exemplified in the previous paragraphs.

3 Metadata in User-Generated Content

> *Haste still pays haste,*
> *and leisure answers leisure;*
> *Like doth quit like,*
> *and Measure still for Measure.*
>> William Shakespeare,
>> Measure for Measure, 1623

As introduced in Subsection 2.1.1, user-generated content units consist of core data and metadata. Core data is the content itself. The content can be text, audio files, pictures, videos or a combination of these. Metadata is information about information. In the context of user-generated content metadata is further information about the content, such as the date of publication or the author of the content.

Users are willing to contribute content as well as metadata on online platforms that allow them to do so (Mika, 2007). Different platforms allow their users to contribute different kinds of metadata. Consequently, user-generated content from different platforms have heterogeneous metadata.

The analysis of metadata for all social media categories is the basis for further insights about the structural nature of user-generated content. To do so it is necessary to collect all features provided by different social media platforms. User-generated content units from different platforms are analyzed. For each category up to 6 representatives were examined. The number of representatives chosen per category depends on how diverse a category's representatives are. If all platforms of a category provide the same information, one example already suffices to show what kind of information is provided by platforms belonging to that category. If there are differences between platforms belonging to the same category, more examples are presented to illustrate the differences.

The following chapter starts with a summary of the analysis of metadata for each category. The second section of this chapter introduces the structural types of metadata that can be observed throughout the categories. The third section introduces a semantic pattern for the metadata of user-generated content. The pattern applies to user-generated content from all categories and is independent of the platform. This is the basis for the modeling of a ranking that works category-independent. A full list of features provided by the social media platforms analyzed can be found in the Appendix.

3.1 Analysis of Metadata for User-Generated Content

This section summarizes the analysis of metadata for user-generated content for each category. It is the basis for further analysis and modeling presented in the subsequent chapters.

3.1.1 Blogs

User-generated content units from blogs are **blog posts**. The traditional blog is written by one single person and blog posts are displayed in reverse chronological order showing the most recent entry on top of the page. Today, blogs occur in many different varieties. They range from personal diaries to professional journalists' and multi-authored blogs.

Whether a blog is single-authored or multi-authored, a single posting always has one author, a publishing date and a source. The source is the blog it was published in. Other than those three, there are no further measures that are standard in blogs. But there is a multitude of useful measures that occur in some blogs. Often found in blogs is a feature that allows readers to comment on blog posts. Every comment shows that the blog entry has been worth a user's time to write the comment. The number of comments on a blog entry indicates that the entry has been noticed. Some blogs also count and display the number of views per entry.

Similar to back-links that are references from other Web sites to the blog, **track-backs** refer to references from other Web sites to a specific posting. The number of track-backs indicates how many others regarded a posting as interesting or useful. Track-backs can only be applied for user-generated content units that have a distinct URL.

The reverse chronological order in which blog posts are displayed could imply that for blogs most recent entries are also the most relevant. But this cannot be generally assumed. There are also blogs about topics that are not dependent on time. Blogs tend to evolve around special topics its authors are interested in and have gathered some expertise in (Macdonald et al., 2010). There are blogs about current events, new products or recent experiences for which the most recent entry indeed tends to be also the most interesting. Blog entries that discuss general ideas or giving advice on problems are less dependent on time. Also, blogs about personal interests, such as photography or literature, are like collections in character. In collections the most recent entry can be as interesting as any other entry. Therefore blogs are often alternatively structured with categories and tags. An example is Wordpress, an open source blogging tool. Wordpress provides tags and categories to group related posts (WordPress, 2013).

For a single-authored blog the rating of the blog is equal to the rating of the author. For a multi-authored blog this is not the case. To

Figure 3.1: Example for a blog post with a plugin from another platform.
The screen-shot shows a blog post with an integrated Flattr button at the bottom (Peter, 2013). The post has been flattred six times, which means that the author of the post receives small amounts of money from six of his readers, who enjoyed the text. The text of the blog post has been shortened and masked to guide the reader's attention.

automatically decide whether a blog is single- or multi-authored is not trivial and can also change over time. Since a posting has a single author and a single source, the information about the author and about the source can be allocated separately to the posting. Thus, postings from single- or multi-authored blogs can be treated alike.

There are approaches that rank blogs. They can be classified as either link-based or feature-driven. They rank whole blogs, not single postings. Therefore, they cannot be directly integrated into the ranking of a content unit. The number of **back-links**—the number of times

Figure 3.2: Example for a blog post with several plugins from other platforms.
The screen-shot shows a blog post with plugins (from left to right) from Twitter, Facebook's *like*, Reddit, Email, Google+, share on Facebook, send to StumbleUpon, *Fark It!*, Share on LinkedIn, and more sharing options in the box at the bottom (Beadon, 2013). The text of the blog post has been shortened and masked to guide the reader's attention.

a blog is referenced—is an example for a simple ranking feature for a whole blog. Link-based blog ranking approaches estimate the relevance of a blog by the number other blogs that link to it. The relevance of a source can be applied to predict the probability for a piece of content published within that platform to be relevant as well.

Some blogs integrate other social media applications as plugins. These plugins can be clicked and have a certain meaning. A click on a Twitter button means that the post is shared on Twitter. A Facebook button means that the post is shared on Facebook. A Facebook *like* button means that the expresses his approval of the text without sharing it. A Flattr[1] button means that the reader of the post donates a small amount of money to the author. Figure 3.1 shows an example of a *flattred* blog post. Figure 3.2 shows an example of a blog that includes various plugins. They allow to *like* a content unit or to share it on social networks. This is also a way to crowd-source relevance.

The following are examples for other social media applications that are currently often used in blogs:

- Flattr[2]
- Twitter
- Facebook (e.g., *share* & *like*)
- Google+[3]
- Stumble[4]
- InShare[5]
- Reddit[6]

---

[1]Flattr is a microdonation provider (`http://flattr.com/`).
[2]`http://flattr.com/`
[3]`http://www.google.com/intl/en/+1/button`
[4]`http://www.stumbleupon.com/`
[5]`http://de.linkedin.com/`
[6]`http://www.reddit.com/`

Each click on a plugin button means that a user consumed the post—at least partly—and rewarded the post with an interaction. The possible interactions can have different semantics that express a higher or lower level of involvement, but they are all human selected recommendations. Human recommendations are a useful source of information for others when they try to select content for their own consumption.

As texts in general, the text of a blog-post can be analyzed with regards to text length, frequency and use of specific words, number of references within the text, and so on.

3.1.2 Forums

A peculiarity of forums is their discussion-like character. This is what makes them so valuable for topics that need debate. But that also often leads to off-topic discussions that make it difficult to find the desired content units.

Forums tend to evolve around specific fields of interest. Forums are particularly valuable for users who seek like minded people, specialists in a field of interest or information about specific topics. Specialists share their knowledge in their field of competence. They also write about their experiences with products and brands. In technologically oriented forums for example computers, monitors, and gadgets are discussed. In telecommunication forums the best service providers and mobile devices are disputed. In sports oriented forums users share recommendations about training and their experiences with the latest sports gear. Hence, forums are also a popular source of product information prior to buying (Elsas & Glance, 2010).

There is a large number of forums with various focus topics online. There are some sources online that provide overviews and statistics for forums, one of which is Big Boards.[7] Most forums are based

---

[7]http://www.big-boards.com

on either phpBB or vBulletin. Phpbb is an open source software,[8] whereas vBulletin has to be licensed.[9] These forum solutions only support a fixed order of topics. Organizing threads or postings by any concept of ranking is not common.

Consequently, the user has to orientate himself by reading through the topics and threads. Most forums also offer a text search that delivers matching results without a particular ranking.

It is especially hard to get an overview over all the information available for a posting published in a forum. This is due to the hierarchical structure of forums. Measures, that are helpful to estimate the relevance of a posting, are distributed among the different levels of a forum's hierarchical structure. Information such as when a posting has been published and by whom it was posted can be found on posting-level as *publishing date* and *author*, as Figure 3.3 shows. The number of views and how many answers there are to an initial posting can be found on thread-level as *number of replies*, as Figure 3.4 shows. The number of threads and postings can be found on topic-level, as Figure 3.5 shows. Information about how many users are active in a forum-community and how many subsequent remarks there are to an initial posting can be found one level above thread level.

A large amount of postings within a topic (or sub-forum) can indicate that a topic is popular. Another reason for a large amount of postings within a topic or sub-forum can also be the way a topic or sub-forum is composed. If for example one sub-forum subsumes all cultural topics, whereas political topics are subdivided into several sub-forums, numbers are difficult to compare. The inner structure of topics of interest is not mandatory. Sub-forums and topics are organized manually and consequently differ in their organization. The difference in topic organization can also be interpreted as a bias, intended by a human mind. The resulting bias in the calculation might therefore be still reasonable in the semantics of the forum and therefore still helpful

---

[8]http://www.phpbb.com
[9]http://www.vbulletin.com

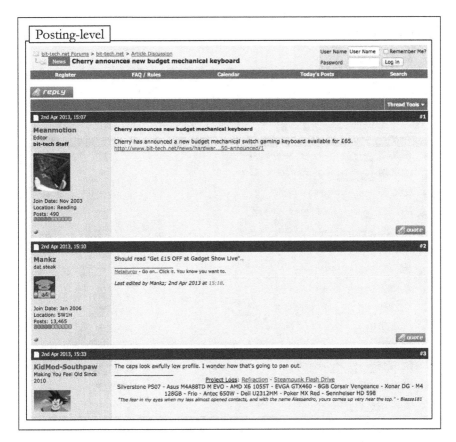

Figure 3.3: Forums' posting-level.
The screen-shot shows the hierarchic structure of forums showing the postings on posting-level, screen-shot from `http://forums.bit-tech.net`, accessed: August 15, 2012.

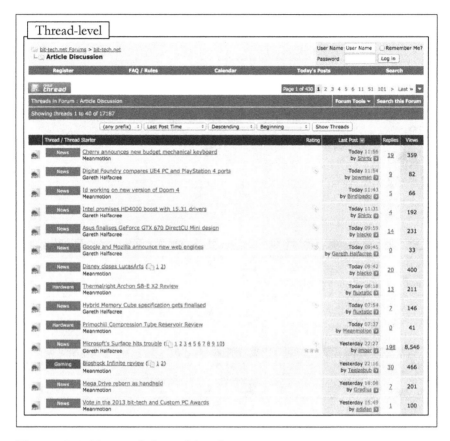

Figure 3.4: Forums' thread-level.
The screen-shot shows the hierarchic structure of forums on
thread-level, screen-shot from `http://forums.bit-tech.`
`net`, accessed: August 15, 2012.

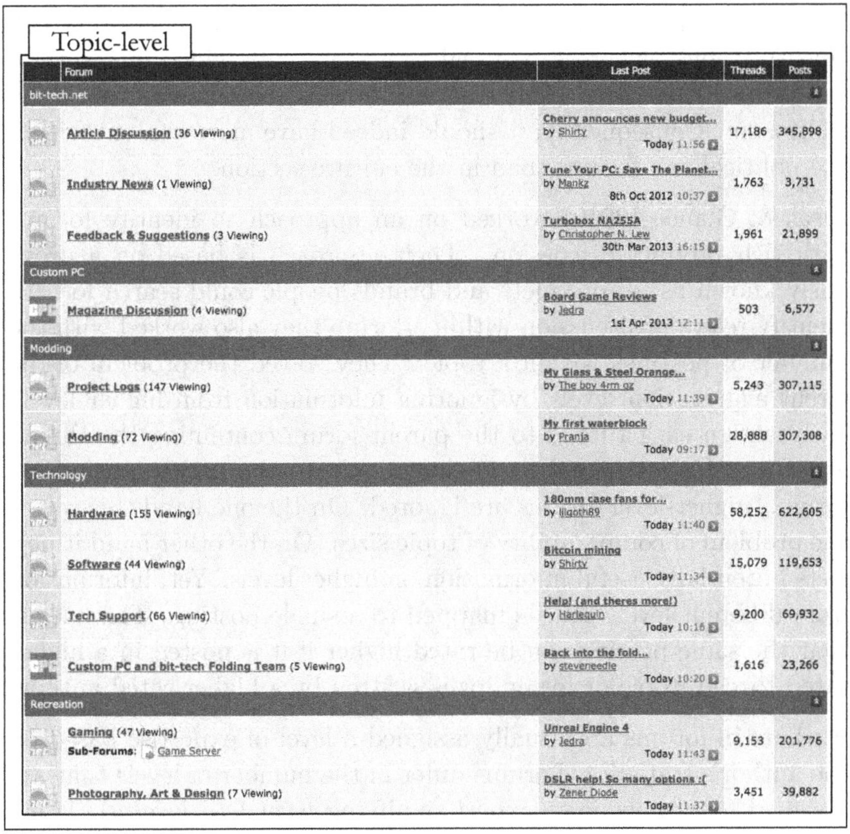

Figure 3.5: Forums' topic-level.
The screen-shot shows the hierarchic structure of forums on topic-level which gives an overview of the forum's topics, screen-shot from `http://forums.bit-tech.net`, accessed: August 15, 2012.

for the user. If for example the above mentioned forum subsumes all cultural topics, whereas political topics are subdivided into several sub-forums, this could likely be a forum that was founded as a political forum. Consequently, it should indeed have more content within the political sub-forums than in the culture section.

Elsas & Glance (2010) worked on an approach to identify forums with rich product discussion. Their approach is based on a previously known list of products and brands people could search for. To identify relevant discussion within a forum they also worked with the number of postings within a topic. They solved the problem of different aggregation levels by ignoring information from higher levels. They assign each thread to the parent forum containing the thread assuming that each message belongs only to the immediate parent forum. Higher-level forums are ignored. On the one hand this solves the problem of comparability of topic sizes. On the other hand it neglects potentially useful information on higher levels. Yet, information from different levels can be mapped to a single posting. This means that the same posting can be rated higher if it is posted in a higher rated thread, topic or forum, or is written by a higher rated author.

Authors in forums are usually assigned a level of expertise based on the author's statistics. Forums differ in the number of levels that are assigned (e.g., *newbie* to *expert* signifying *level 1* to *level n*). Users who are new to a forum-community are mostly users who search for expertise. They initially become a member to post their questions. In contrast, users who are members for a longer time, are more likely to be interested in the topic of the forum in general. The number of postings published by an author can be interpreted as indicator for expertise presuming that a user who posts more has more expertise to share. The duration of his membership in combination with his activity derived from the date of his last posting gives further allusion to his potential to publish useful content.

3.1.3 Location Sharing and Annotation Platforms

Location sharing and annotation refers to collaboratively produced metadata for virtual representations of physical places. Foursquare,[10] Loopt,[11] Facebook Places,[12] and Google Latitude[13] are examples for location sharing and annotation platforms. These applications are rapidly growing. Foursquare has more than 15 million users[14] and Facebook places is used by more than 30 million users. Users of Foursquare shared their locations over a 100 million times by July 2010 (Cramer et al., 2011, p. 57).

Location-sharing services have a longer history in research then they are available for consumers. Research activities with focus on locating and tracking people go back to the early 1990s (Pier, 1991; Harper, Lamming & Newman, 1992). The first locator technology was the ActiveBadge, originated at Olivetti Cambridge Research Lab. It was intended for office application. Badges should be worn in the workplace to track locations of employees. Even at this early point of research sociological and ethical questions were raised and considered important. The questions posed by Pier (1991, p. 285) "Will 'Big Brother' monitor your every move?" and "Can we architect systems that provide desirable services without actually revealing any individual's location and trail unless given permission by that individual?" illustrate farsightedness as well as the core problem with location tracking systems. Most ensuing systems in research have focused on location tracking, while providing the user with different levels of control over what is shared with whom, usually a limited audience (Iachello, Smith, Consolvo, Chen & Abowd, 2005; Reilly, Dearman, Ha, Smith & Inkpen, 2006; Barkhuus, Brown, Bell, Sherwood, Hall & Chalmers, 2008; Scellato, Noulas, Lambiotte & Mascolo, 2011).

---

[10]https://de.foursquare.com
[11]http://www.loopt.com
[12]https://www.facebook.com/about/location
[13]http://www.google.com/latitude
[14]https://foursquare.com/about

**Figure 3.6: Representation of the New York Marriott Marquis
Hotel on the location sharing and annotation platform Foursquare.**
Foursquare (2013) gives general information about the venue
such as address and contact information. Users uploaded
1879 photos of the hotel. They can be accessed at the top of
the page. Below the short text about the hotel the number
of total visitors and the number of check-ins is displayed.
Visitors left tips for other users, which are displayed at the
bottom of the page.

Figure 3.7: A user's profile on on the location sharing and annotation platform Foursquare.

In the profile the user, Daer (2013), presents information about herself. At the top her name is displayed along with a short text describing herself. This user has performed 6,014 check-ins and given 174 tips, one of which is the New York Marriott Marquis Hotel in Figure 3.6. On the right hand side the number of *badges*, the user's level ("Superuser Level 1") and the number of her *mayorships* are displayed. At the bottom right the number of friends is provided. This view of this user's profile is general public as specified in Section 2.1.1 (see also Figure 2.1 on page 15). It can be accessed without being a member of Foursquare.

The question "Can we architect systems that provide desirable services without actually revealing any individual's location and trail unless given permission by that individual?" (Pier, 1991, p. 285) already contains the answer to the addressed problem: permission by the individual. The important issue regarding privacy is that the location sharing is performed manually and not via tracking. Current solutions do not automatically track and share peoples' location. If desired by the individual user, he can give permission and reveal his location to others. Each publication is enabled and authorized by the user himself. In in-depth interviews Cramer et al. (2011) observed a shift from privacy concern driven behavior and data deluge to performative considerations in location sharing.

Check-ins are manually entered to pair user location with semantically enriched venues (e.g., restaurants, grocery stores, bars), which are visible to other users. Figure 3.6 shows an example of the representation of a hotel on the location sharing and annotation platform Foursquare.

The venues are the central reference points in location sharing and annotation. A venue has a name and a geographical location. Furthermore, the total number people who have visited a location so far is provided along with the total number of *check-ins*. Assuming that users rather share places they like with other people, a large number of visitors suggest a high popularity of a location. A high ratio of *check-ins* per visitor suggests loyal customers. Annotations of locations always have an author and a publishing date. Users can rate the annotations of other users.

Additionally, the location sharing and annotation-user's profile shows how many total *check-ins* she published so far and how long she has been active on the platform. Figure 3.7 shows an example of a user's profile on the location sharing and annotation platform Foursquare.

3.1.4 Media Sharing Platforms

Media sharing platforms are platforms where registered users can upload content and share it with friends or provide it to the public. Existing platforms are specialized on specific media such as pictures, videos or audio content. Youtube is the most successful platform of our times for video sharing.[15] Flickr is an example for a platform where users share pictures.[16]

Users can connect with other users. Connections can be unidirectional as typical for microblogs or mutual. Youtube even supports both types of relationships, namely *friends* and *subscribers*. Flickr supports friends as well as groups users can join. Usually, the number of connections is lower than in social networks. This might be due to the fact that in social media sharing platforms users do not have to be connected to see each others content. Users can comment on the content and contribute one-click-opinions.

A user-generated content unit from a social media sharing site usually has a contributor, a publishing date, a number of one-click-opinions, a number of views and a number of comments. Figure 3.8 and Figure 3.9 show examples of content units from two different social media sharing platforms.

User profiles typically give information about the user's nickname, the date when the user became member of the community, and the number of content units contributed.

3.1.5 Microblogs

In microblogs the author does not specify a recipient. The reader chooses which authors he would like to read postings from. Every message is public by default and the recipients choose whose messages they read. The *follow* relation is not mutual.

---

[15]http://www.youtube.com
[16]http://www.flickr.com

Figure 3.8: A user-generated content unit on the media sharing platform Youtube.

The screen-shot shows an example for a user-generated content unit on Youtube. The platform displays the video in the main area. It shows the title of the video *120715 - PSY - Gangnam style (Comeback stage)...* and the contributing user CapsuleHD20 (2012). Furthermore, the number of views and the number of user ratings are displayed. The bottom of the figure page shows when the video has been contributed. In this example, the contributor is not the artist of the video. The artist—PSY—is explicitly named at the right side of the bottom of the screen-shot.

**Figure 3.9: A user-generated content unit on the media sharing
platform Flickr.**
The screen-shot shows an example for a user-generated content unit on Flickr (Garlesteanu, 2013). The platform displays the picture in the main area. Below the picture is the
title *rusty scissor* and the nickname of the contributing user
Garlesteanu Cosmin. Furthermore, the platform shows that
this picture has been given 102 *favorites* and 27 comments.
During the three days since it has been taken, it has been
viewed 4,141 times.

Twitter is a typical representative. A *tweet* has always one distinct author and a publishing date. *Favorites* are Twitter's one-click-opinions.
Tweets can be further distributed by other users. For Twitter this is
called *retweet*. The number of *favorites* and the number of *retweets*
are displayed with the content unit. They help users to estimate the
importance of a tweet.

The user's profile information shows how many content units a user
contributed, how many *followers* he has and how many others he
follows (i.e., *following*). The number of *followers* indicates an author's
reach. The more *followers* an author has, the more people consider

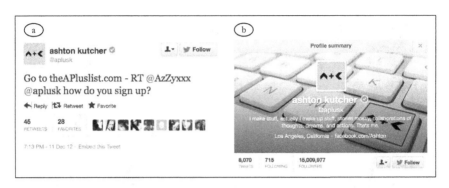

Figure 3.10: A user-generated content unit and a user's profile on Twitter.
a: **A user-generated content unit published on Twitter.** Below the text, the number of *retweets*, the number of *favorites*, and the date of publication is displayed. Above the text, the author of the user-generated content unit is displayed.
b: **A user's profile.** The author, Kutcher (2013), provides a picture and a nickname. He wrote two sentences about himself, reveals where he lives and provides an additional link. The profile shows that this user has contributed 8,070 content units, that he follows 715 other users, and that 15,010,002 users follow him.

his contributions worth reading. If we think about the author and his *followers* as a directed graph, more conclusions about the value of an author's *followers* can be drawn. A user who follows fewer authors could be considered to be more selective about content and to choose more carefully whom he follows. Furthermore, it could be assumed that this user is more likely to really read the postings by those authors. The conclusion can now be drawn that a large number of *followers* who follow many authors is not as valuable as having the same amount of *followers* who follow a small number of authors. Figure 3.10 shows an example of a user-generated content unit and a user's profile from the microblogging platform Twitter. Microblogs differ from traditional blogs in being much shorter and smaller in file size. For example, a *tweet* is limited to 140 characters. It contains text sometimes accompanied by a short-link.[17] Therefore, the length of *tweets* varies only in this small range. A particularity of microblogs is that there are syntax agreements, which can be used within the text. The syntax is not technically imposed by Twitter. It has emerged as conventions from the users' needs. Category tags could be derived from the text itself as well by parsing for the number sign (#). *Retweets* can easily be parsed, since they are marked within the text message by the letters *RT*.

3.1.6 Question and Answer Platforms

In question and answer platforms users can pose questions and other users can answer them. Question and answer platforms usually allow peer-ratings. Answers can be rated by other users. The goal of the rating procedure is to find the best, ideally the correct answer from all answers given.

Questions as well as answers have a publishing date and an author. The author's profile usually shows the author's nickname, *membership since*, the number of contributions, the number of questions posed, the number of questions answered, and the number of—usually peer-rated—*best answers*.

According to the works of Agichtein et al. (2008), the most significant indicators for the quality of questions as well as answers are peer ratings. Other significant features for quality classification of questions and answers are features derived from text analysis, such as punctuation density in the question's subject, number of words per sentence, the number of capitalization errors in the question, answer length (rewarding longer texts), unique number of words in an answer, and the word overlap between the question and the answer.

---

[17] A short-link is a URL that is shortened in length and still directs to the required page.

3.1.7 Rating and Review Platforms

Rating and review platforms are specialized for ratings and reviews of products, services or experiences. Ratings and reviews can also be part of commercial platforms. Amazon is an example for a commercial platform that allows ratings and reviews by users. Content of this type is also referred to as **consumer-generated product reviews** (Archak, Ghose & Ipeirotis, 2007) or **online consumer reviews** (Yu, Zha, Wang & Chua, 2011).

For ratings and reviews the author as well as the date of publishing are displayed to the reader. Reviews are written texts of flexible length. Sometimes pictures can be contributed as well. Ratings are one-click-opinions on different scales. Some platforms offer several one-click-opinions for predefined criteria. Sometimes users who are willing to contribute a review have to provide their ratings for all of the predefined criteria offered. On one hand, this can have the advantage that ratings are more differentiated. On the other hand, the predefined criteria need to fit the object of the rating which is not always the case.[18]

Furthermore, most platforms allow peer-ratings of the reviews. Platforms differ in the scales they offer. Some offer a binary scale *This review was helpful to me.* and *This review was not helpful to me.* (e.g., Amazon). Others offer to rate the degree of helpfulness on several levels (e.g., Ciao). Figure 3.11 shows an example of a user-generated content unit and a user's profile from the rating and review platform Ciao.

To give readers information about the author of a review, the number of *helpfuls* is displayed along with the review itself. A high number of positive peer-ratings indicates a high quality review.

---

[18]For example, Ciao.de makes reviewers rate the smell of electronic products, such as an electric toothbrush (Ciao, 2013). *Smell* as rating criterion might be suitable for toothpaste, but is irritating for an electric toothbrush.

Figure 3.11: A user-generated content unit and a user's profile on the rating and review platform Ciao.
a: A user-generated content unit published on Ciao. Next to the author's nickname and her profile picture, is the overall rating the author gave the product (RosesAreRed1207, 2012). She rated the iPhone 5 with four out of five stars. Below this a short summary of advantages and disadvantages are given and the review can be accessed. The review has been published on November 6, 2012. On this platform other members can rate reviews on a six-level scale from *off-topic* through *helpful* to *exceptional*. Other users have rated this review on average *exceptional*.
b: User's profile. The user's profile shows additional information. In this case, we learn that the author has been member of the Ciao-community since May 11, 2011. During that time she has written 752 reviews. This platform allows members to select other members they trust and form a network of trustees. The trust relationship is not mutual. This author is trusted by 68 members.

Sometimes, users can also comment on reviews. In this case, the number of comments a review received is displayed.

Most platforms require a registration to contribute reviews. Authors can register with a pseudonym or their real name. Some systems offer to confirm the correctness of the real name (e.g., Amazon). Authors' profiles are publicly accessible providing statistics about the user's reviews to other users. The statistics differ from platform to platform. All platforms display the number of reviews the user has contributed. If peer-ratings are offered, the average peer-rating the author received for his reviews is commonly displayed, too. Some systems offer detailed statistics about peer-ratings and contributions (e.g., Ciao shows *number of readings received, number of comments received, number of comments written*, etc.).

3.1.8 Social Networks

Social networks are characterized by their users and the connections between them. Connections can be either mutual as the *friends* connection in Facebook or unidirectional as it is in Google's social network Google+. Google+ users can add anyone to their *circles* (i.e., the user's networks), the other user does not confirm the connection. For each publication users can specify to which circle they like to publish it.

A user-generated content unit is always published with author and date of publication. A user-generated content unit is published in a social network as part of so-called feeds. Usually, a user-generated content unit appears in the feeds of all users connected with the contributor. Therefore, the number of connections indicates a user's reach. Originally, those postings consisted of short text messages. The possibilities to post photos, links and videos were added gradually. Usually, people can rate entries by leaving one-click-opinions, comment on it and share content with their connections. This leads to a number of further measures, such as number of one-click-opinions, number of comments, and number of shares. Figure 3.12 shows two examples of user-generated content units from social networks.

For the purpose of this work it is important to note that content published in social networks might be published only to the limited public. If content is not published to the general public, it should not be analyzed, except the reader is included in a limited public.

3.2 Cross-Category Comparison of Metadata

After appraisal of all the measures that occur in different social media categories, the data can be analyzed for patterns. To develop a modeling concept that provides comparability of information, the collected measures are analyzed for similarities and differences across the categories.

First of all, the elements that are to be ranked need to be determined. This decides also on which level user-generated content is compared. For user-generated content that stands for itself—that is, it does not refer to other elements and does not have other elements referring to them—this is straightforward. But for a product review for example, it needs to be specified whether the products, the review, or the comment to the review should be ranked.

It is necessary to distinguish the object of a user-generated content unit (e.g., that can be a product on a rating and review platform or a location on a location sharing and annotation platform), the central user-generated content unit, and the user-generated content units that refer to the content unit as comments. Figure 3.13 illustrates this structure. It shows the central user-generated content unit as contribution in the middle (labeled 1.). A contribution has an author, a source and a publishing date. A contribution can have comments (labeled 2.). A comment can have an author, too. But in the context of this work it is interpreted as additional information about a contribution. It is not object of the ranking itself. A contribution can

**Figure 3.12: User-generated content units from the social net-
works Google+ and Facebook.**
The screen-shots show the information that is visible to the
unregistered user. Both platforms show the author and the
publishing date of the user-generated content units. Furthermore, both allow to comment on the content and share
it with others. The platforms also reveal who liked, shared
and commented on the content units, even to users who are
not member of the social networks.
**a: A user-generated content unit published on
Google+.** The content unit has received 382 *+1*—
Google's one-click-opinions—so far (Lobo, 2013b).
**b: A user-generated content unit published on Face-
book.** The content unit has received 292 *likes*—Facebook's
one-click-opinions—so far (Lobo, 2013a).

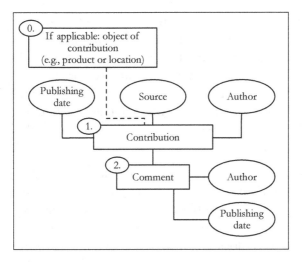

Figure 3.13: User-generated content and the allocation of information.
The boxes labeled 0.–2. represent content. It can be text, pictures or other media. The ellipses represent metadata. In the center of consideration is the contribution (1.). The contribution has a publishing date, a source, an author. The contribution can have comments allocated to it (2.). A comment also has an author and usually a publishing date. The contribution can have an object it refers to (0.). For rating and review platforms that can be a product for example.

refer to other objects (labeled 0. in Figure 3.13). In the context of this work, this is also not object of the ranking.

For each social media category analyzed in Section 3.1, there is a level of granularity for which there is a publishing date, a source where it has been published and an author by whom it was published. In the context of this work, this is the object of the ranking and the level of comparison. It correlates to the contribution in Figure 3.13.

Three basic types of information can be distinguished: content information, primary information, and secondary information.

Content information is information derived from the content. For example, if a social media content unit contains text, the text itself can be parsed to derive further information. Simple examples are text length, number of words and sentences or number of question marks or the number of links the text contains. Less simple examples are the numbers of previously defined strings or positive and negative adjectives. For videos, this can be the file size or the duration of the video.

Primary information is information that is displayed directly on the level with the user-generated content unit. It refers directly to one content unit. The publishing date and the author of a content are examples of information that is always displayed with the content unit (i.e., the user does not have to navigate). Publishing date and author refer to a content unit and can be distinctly allocated.

Secondary information is information that refers to information about a user-generated content unit. Secondary information is often found on a different level than the content unit itself. It can refer to more than one content unit. The number of content units an author has contributed is an example for secondary information. It reveals information about the author and cannot be directly allocated to a content unit. But, if we know who the author of a content unit is and we know something about the author, we can draw conclusions about the content units the author publishes.

Secondary information, allocated to a user-generated content unit, can be differentiated according to the roots of heritage. Information derived from the thread of a user-generated content unit from a forum is **thread inherited information** (e.g., number of *views* of a thread). **Source-related information** is secondary information that is derived from the source of a social media content unit (e.g., number of community members). **Author-related information** is secondary information that is derived from an author's profile (e.g., number of *best answers* an author contributed).

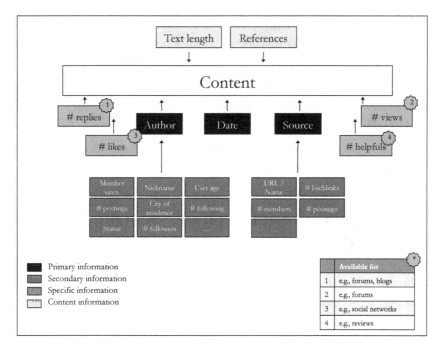

Figure 3.14: Types of information for user-generated content units.

User-generated content units consist of content and further information. Author, date, and source are primary information. Secondary information is further information about primary information. Specific information is available for some platforms for others not. Content information is information derived from the content.

There is source-related information that can be assessed for all categories. An example is the number of back-links to a source. There is also source-related information that is specific for certain categories. The number of members of a community in a social network is an example. Similarly, there are different kinds of author-related information that can be assessed through the author's profile, depending on the platform. Microblogs for example offer the number of followers and the total number of tweets, whereas forums show the number

of contributions without number of followers since that concept does
not exist in forums. Nevertheless, both examples reveal further information about the author.

Specific information occurs only on certain platforms. Specific
information is not available for all types of user-generated content.
Various forms of peer-ratings are examples.

Figure 3.14 shows an overview of all types of information related to
a user-generated content unit.

3.3 From Data to Information: Semantics of Metadata

A datum without a meaning is just a number. When data have
meaning, it becomes information that is useful for humans. Focus of
the following section is the interpretation of the metadata available
for user-generated content.

3.3.1 Why It Matters Who the Author Is

Conducting information from an author to his assertions is a well-
known concept. If someone likes the novel *Great Expectations*, he
might want to read *David Copperfield* as well, because it is also a
novel by Charles Dickens. Of course, it may happen that one novel
of an author is excellent and another is not. But, although we cannot
draw conclusions that are reliable in every case, it is an approximation
that proved efficient for the majority of cases.

Expertism is another example of how the reputation of an author is
used to draw conclusions about the content he or she produces. In
traditional media, an example for trusted experts are journalists. An
article written by a journalist is expected to be of better quality than
an article by a layman. The same applies for scientists and their

publications. An academic degree increases the trustworthiness of a contribution to a discourse induced by assumed expertism. In science, authors are more likely to be cited if they have already been cited more often than comparable work. A highly rewarded scientist who has published many well respected works is expected to publish more work that deserves respect. Quoting this well respected author will probably be more convincing than quoting someone unknown. If someone announces the consumption of onions would relieve migraine symptoms, more people will try it if that someone is a neurology professor, than if that someone is an organic farmer. These conclusions are not necessarily correct for every single publication. But nevertheless, even though it is not precise, it is an efficient approximation.

With the advent of social media, readers are confronted with many authors; more than they could ever learn enough about to judge their content by their reputation. Some users might have the feeling that this mass of authors contributing content in social media virtually equals complete anonymity. But, there is information about authors in social media, too. An author who has written several contributions has proved his loyalty over the last years of his membership, whereas for an author who has just joined a community it is unknown whether he only joined the community to fake positive reviews about his own products. An author who has many followers has probably a higher reach than an author who has just a few. An author who received many *best answer* peer-ratings for his answers is probably more reliable than an author who has just contributed his first answer.

Authors' profiles vary significantly in the amount of personal information provided. There are authors who provide profile pictures, real names, contact information, and even provide the link to their personal Web site, whereas other authors provide a nickname only. Studies suggest that Web site credibility is enhanced by providing personal and contact information (Fogg, Marshall, Laraki, Osipovich, Varma, Fang, Paul, Rangnekar, Shon, Swani & Treinen, 2001; Fogg, Marshall, Osipovich, Varma, Laraki, Fang, Paul, Rangnekar, Shon, Swani et al., 2000; Fogg, Soohoo, Danielson, Marable, Stanford & Tauber, 2003).

3.3.2 Why It Matters Where Something Is Published

The source of a publication allows to draw conclusions about the publication itself. Properties of a source can be applied to predict the probability for a piece of content published within that platform to have these properties as well. This concept is well established. It is a concept known to users from traditional media.

Newspapers, book publishers, television channels are examples. When a reader decides to buy a newspaper, there are expectations about its contents. Political orientations and sophistication are examples. The quality and credibility of an article can be roughly classified by the kind of newspaper it is published in. If an article is published in The New York Times for example, readers probably expect it to be more credible and of higher quality than an article from a boulevard magazine.

Further conclusions can be drawn from a newspapers reach. A local newspaper covers different stories than an international newspaper. And if a story is published in a newspaper with a high run, the news it contains will probably reach more people.

Social media platforms vary widely in their size. The size of a platform can be measured by number of contributions and number of members or visitors. The number of visitors correlates with the potential reach of the platform's content. A message being shared through Twitter—a platform that has 200 million active users (Wickre, 2013)—has a higher potential reach than a message published in a small forum that has 5,000 members. The number of incoming links is an indicator of the probability that the *random surfer*[19] visits the platform and an indicator of its relative importance (Page et al., 1998). The probability is higher that users read an article accidentally if it is published on a platform that has many

---

[19]The random surfer is a notion used by Page et al. (1998). The random surfer surfs the Web by randomly following its hyperlink structure. When he arrives at a page with several outlinks, he randomly chooses one, navigates to the new page and continues this process indefinitely (Langville & Meyer, 2006).

incoming links than if it is published on an unnoticed personal blog that has no incoming links. The mechanism can be compared to the print run of newspapers. An article published in a small local newspaper is less likely to be spread than an article published in a widely read international newspaper.

3.3.3 What the Content Reveals

User-generated content can consist of texts, pictures, video, and audio files, or a mixture of them. Often, nontext multi-media content is also accompanied by descriptive text.

Text can be analyzed for text features that are known to correlate with characteristics of the text. Studies show that citations, references and other kinds of source material contribute to a text's credibility (Fogg et al., 2000, 2001). Links within the text of a user-generated content unit can help to ascertain the source of information and indicate utility as they point to additional sources of information that can help the user (Moturu, 2010; Elgersma & de Rijke, 2008). Quotation marks are an indicator for citations as well, but they are also commonly used to indicate irony. A solution for the disambiguation of quotation marks used for irony and quotation marks used for citations could be that, in the case of irony, typically only one or two words are set in quotation marks, whereas a quotation is usually longer.

There are also machine learning algorithms that can be applied to detect quality flaws. Anderka et al. propose an approach for automatic quality flaw detection for Wikipedia articles. They propose to interpret the detection of quality flaws as one-class classification problem identifying articles that contain a particular quality flaw among a set of articles. An example for a frequent quality flaw is not citing any references or sources in an article (Anderka, Stein & Lipka, 2011b). The texts that contain a particular quality flaw are given as positive examples to decide for unseen texts whether they contain that particular flaw. For each known flaw, an expert is asked whether a

given document suffers from it. Based on the manually tagged document set, for each flaw a one-class classifier is evaluated, trained, and
tested.

The automatic determination of text quality is object of many research projects (e.g., Chen, Liu, Chang & Lee, 2010; Kakkonen,
Myller, Timonen & Sutinen, 2005). Typically, these approaches analyze texts for predefined vocabulary and text structure. Predefined
vocabulary is not applicable to the task at hand. First of all, it is
typical for user-generated content that neologisms and abbreviations
are used. Furthermore, vocabulary is language-dependent and the
work at hand aims at a language-independent approach. For the
automated quality assessment of Wikipedia articles Dalip, Gonçalves,
Cristo & Calado (2009) show that text length as well as structure and
style are the most important quality features. Text length is a feature often used as quality indicator (e.g., Moturu, 2010; Dalip et al.,
2009; Hu et al., 2007). Concerns are that text structure is not applicable to all types of user-generated content, because there are no
common conveniences for text structure that apply to all platforms
under consideration.

Which metrics are used to determine the quality of content is a choice
that also needs to be based on the desired accuracy and the available resources. Text length is a feature that can be easily extracted,
whereas a classification approach requires more processing resources.

3.3.4 What Other People Tell Us

"Under the right circumstances, groups are remarkably intelligent,
and are often smarter than the smartest people in them." (Surowiecki,
2005, p. XIII). The **wisdom of the crowds** phenomenon refers to the
observation that the aggregated solutions from a group of individuals
are sometimes better than the majority of the individual solutions.
Traditionally, it has been applied to point estimation of continuous-
valued physical quantities for example (Surowiecki, 2005). The use of

the wisdom of the crowds is an emerging field of research. It has also been widely applied for discrete labeling (Raykar, Yu, Zhao, Valadez, Florin, Bogoni & Moy, 2010), the prediction of urban traffic routes (Yu, Low, Oran & Jaillet, 2012), and Web page clipping (Zhang, Tang, Luo, Chen, Jiao, Wang & Liu, 2012). Wisdom of the crowds can be applied to assist individuals in their decision making process by gathering data about the decisions taken by a group of individuals.

For social media, every one-click-opinion—every *thumbs up*, every *like*, every *+1*, and so on—is an assessment of a content unit. Each interaction—be it a one-click-opinion of any kind or a comment— with a content unit means that a user felt that a content unit was worth spending time with it. User interactions with a contribution are a valuable source of information for other users who search for interesting content. Mishne & Glance (2006) demonstrate that the number of comments is a strong indicator for the popularity of a blog post. Compared to a comment, the amount of time a user invests is relatively small when he contributes a one-click-opinion. But, a one-click-opinion is an explicit expression of opinion. The more people consider a content unit is worth an interaction, the higher is the probability that the content unit might be interesting for other users as well. The collection of all user interactions with a content unit is a crowd sourced assessment of the content unit that can serve as recommendation for other users.

3.4 The Social Media Document View

The **social media document view** comprises the structure all user-generated content units have in common.[20] Traditionally, the term

---

[20] The modeling approach presented here is based on the analysis of the metadata of the evaluated platforms. The platforms have been chosen as representatives that cover the typical range for the analyzed categories to allow transferability of results. However, when statements are made about how platforms or platform categories function, it is not impossible that there are or there will be platforms for which the statements do not apply. The descriptions of plat-

document is used to refer to a unit of information, typically consisting of text. It can also contain other media. A document can be a whole book, an article, or be part of a larger text such as a paragraph, a section or a chapter. Here, the term *social media document* has been chosen paralleling traditional information retrieval, where the ranked units are also referred to as *documents*.

Based on the patterns revealed by the cross-category analysis, further conclusions can be drawn for a social media document. I propose a social media specific document view for user-generated content units.

A social media document always has a certain structure that is independent from the category it belongs to. The user-generated content unit always contains content. This can be text, pictures, audio or video files or a combination of them. Measures derived from the content itself are in the following referred to as **intrinsic information**. An example for intrinsic information is the number of references (i.e., links) a text contains.

Metadata about the content on the level of primary information is **extrinsic information**. Examples for extrinsic information are the number of replies and the number of *likes*.

Secondary information that is not specific to a category but is equally provided throughout all social media categories leads to two further elements of the social media document: author-related information and source-related information (cf., Section 3.2). Author-related information can be assessed through the author's identifier (e.g., the author's nickname concatenated to the source name). Source-related information is information about the source and can be assessed through the source's identifier (e.g., its URL).

This is the structure all user-generated content units have in common. Figure 3.15 illustrates the structure. Within the elements of

---

forms and patterns are empirical observations of the platforms as they were at the time of the development of this work. The presented approach has been designed aiming at robustness towards variation and changes, but nevertheless, it does make no claim to be universally valid.

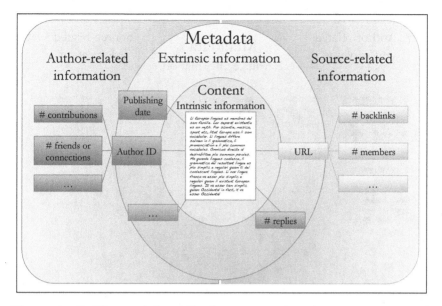

Figure 3.15: The social media document view for user-generated content.
The social media document view comprises the structure all user-generated content units have in common. Measures that can be derived from the content itself are intrinsic information. Metadata about the content is extrinsic information. Information that is not directly about the content unit, but about its author is author-related information. Information about the platform, where the content unit is published on, is source-related information.

the structure the measures may differ depending on the category of the platform. Figure 3.16 illustrates the modeling concept using the example of forum postings.

Traditionally, Web pages are seen as parts of the network World Wide Web. A network can be described as a graph consisting of nodes and edges. In this case, the nodes are Web pages and the edges are the links. Link-based ranking approaches such as the PageRank are based on this view, but do not go beyond the granularity of the Web

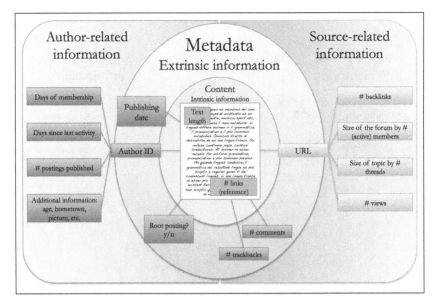

Figure 3.16: Social media document view for forums.
A forum's user-generated content unit has author-related information such as *days of membership* and *number of postings* published. It has information about the post itself, such as the *publishing date* and the *number of comments*. Source-related information for forums are back-links, the *number of active members* in the forum's community, *topic size*, and so on.

page. User-generated content units are parts of web pages and are not considered in this view. Hence, the traditional site-centered view does not apply to user-generated content. I prose a different view—the social media document view—that is adequate for the required granularity of user-generated content.

The social media document view takes into account that one Web page can contain different user-generated content units published by several authors at various times with varying quality. It shifts the focus from the Web page to the content unit. Furthermore, the social media document view accounts for the user's role. In the traditional site-centered view the user does not occur. It was not necessary because the former role of the user was one of passive consumption. Nowadays, the user can actively participate. The World Wide Web of today is significantly co-authored by users. It consists of users acting either as authors publishing content or as readers consuming the content. The user's passive role has shifted to the active role of a contributor. With the author-related information as inherent part of the modeling, the social media document view accounts for that development.

4 Towards Query-Independent Ranking

Two roads diverged in a wood, and I —
I took the one less traveled by

Robert Lee Frost, 1916

The goal of information retrieval is to provide a user with the information he seeks. The information the user desires is referred to as **information need.** The technique with which a retrieval system chooses documents and presents them to the user is referred to as **information retrieval method.** The documents the retrieval system chooses from a larger set of documents in the retrieval process are the **retrieved documents.** Which documents are retrieved depends on the information retrieval method applied. Whether the retrieved documents satisfy the user, depends on his information need. Consequently, the choice of the proper information retrieval method depends on the information need the system is designed for.

To design a retrieval system that satisfies its users there are three main parts to consider: the information need, the information retrieval method, and the objects of retrieval. The following chapter examines this threefold complex. After the introduction of the different kinds of information needs in Section 4.1, I shall point out that traditional information retrieval focuses on a limited number of information needs which can be formulated in a search term. Section 4.2

gives an overview of information retrieval methods. Section 4.3 explains the specifics of user-generated documents and why the known query-independent concepts do not suffice for user-generated content. Moreover, advantages of query-independent ranking methods specifically for user-generated content shall be discussed.

4.1 User Information Needs and Search Strategies

There is a variety of information needs a user can have. In a library a reader can be looking for a book a friend recommended to him. The strategy he should apply to find the book recommended by his friend depends on the information he has about the book. He might know the title or the author. With this information he can retrieve exactly the book he is looking for. This is an example of **known-item search**. The user knows about the existence of the item he is looking for. It can be a specific book in the library or a specific file on his hard drive. Alternatively, the reader could be looking for a book about how to feed red pandas. This case is less straightforward. The searcher has to articulate keywords that represent the topic. Then he can try to find a book on the desired topic by matching the search terms with the title of the book or its content. Maybe the library offers topic related sections, which help to find books about certain topics. This is an example of **topical search**. The user knows what he wants to know. This knowledge helps him to articulate search terms. A reader might also come to the library with the desire to read the book read by the most people. There is no search term that expresses her information need. She can not just search for "the most read book." The books that match this search query will probably not be the most read books. The only chance to find the most popular book is if the library kept information about how many times a book has been borrowed and then look for the one with the highest number of lendings. This type of search is different from the other two. There is no keyword or search query that expresses this information need. Those types of information needs are not specific to common bibliographic systems.

Information needs can be classified according to if and how straightforward they can be expressed as search term. We differentiate between information needs that can easily be expressed as search term and information needs that cannot be expressed as search term. **Content-related information needs** can easily be transferred into a search term. An example is the information need "The book with the title *How to Feed Pandas*." The corresponding search term can be derived from the known title of the book. Another example is the information need "What has been written about Lindsey Vonn?" The corresponding search term could be "Lindsey Vonn." **Feature-related information needs** are not transferable into a search query. Examples are: "What is the most important news of today?" and "What do people talk most about?" In practice, feature-related information needs and content-related information needs can often occur in conjunction. An example would be: "What is the most important news about Lindsey Vonn?"

Feature-related information needs are the types of questions that a user should be able to ask in the context of user-generated content. Additionally, content-related information needs are well studied. There are many approaches that can be applied to user-generated content. Feature-related information needs on the other hand are not that well studied and there are no approaches that are easily applicable to user-generated content. This work will focus on the feature-related information needs.

Different information needs require different search strategies. Search strategies can be classified into two main types: exploratory search and nonexploratory search (Baeza-Yates, Boldi, Bozzon, Brambilla, Ceri & Pasi, 2011). In a **nonexploratory search** the user knows what he wants, whereas **exploratory search** is often applied when the user does not have an exact idea of what he wants to find.

There are several different terms used to describe nonexploratory
search strategies, such as *finding facts*, *satisfy information queries*
(Marchionini & Shneiderman, 1988, p. 70 seqq.), and *complex search*
(Baeza-Yates et al., 2011). Marchionini (2006, p. 42) describes nonexploratory search as "look up search tasks" which comprises fact retrieval, known item search, navigation, transaction, verification, and
question answering. When users perform a nonexploratory search,
they usually know exactly what they are looking for. They have a
clear picture of what a satisfying result will look like and can express
their search intention. The search is planned in advance. Terms
and logical connectives can be systematically combined. It may be a
specific source, author, title, subject, and so on the user has in mind.

In an exploratory search, users do not know exactly what they are
looking for. Exploratory search is also referred to as *browsing* or
browsing knowledge. This information seeking strategy is appropriate for ill-defined problems and to explore new task domains. It
includes *search to learn* and *search to investigate*. Search to learn
comprises information seeking activities such as knowledge acquis-
ition, comprehension, aggregation and social search, where people
aim to find communities of interest. Search to investigate includes
accretion, analysis, synthesis, evaluation, discovery, planning, and
transformation. All these search activities require human participation in a more exploratory and less formalized process. (Marchionini,
2006)

To sum it up, there are different information needs a user can have.
There are also different search strategies a user can follow and there
are different information retrieval methods that can be implemented in the system. Some information needs can be converted into a
search term. Those information needs can be satisfied by search engines that are based on and optimized in query matching approaches.
But, there are information needs that can not be transferred to a
search term. Those require different approaches. Information need
and search strategy are user related, and the information retrieval
method is system related. The information need and the retrieval

method are fixed in a given situation. If information need and retrieval strategy are not appropriate for each other, the only variable
the user can adapt to the situation is his search strategy. The user
can adjust his search strategy only as much as the system enables it.
To support exploratory search, Marchionini (2006) proposes that the
search interface should allow more human interaction in the search
process. I suggest to consider the information retrieval strategies with
regard to the information needs that can be satisfied with them. The
following section introduces information retrieval strategies.

4.2 Query-Dependent and Query-Independent Ranking

Generally speaking, information retrieval is about finding information (Goker & Davies, 2009). Information retrieval aims at finding
material of an unstructured nature that satisfies an information need
from within large collections, usually stored on computers (Manning,
Raghavan & Schütze, 2008). This field of study has a relatively long
tradition. Already in 1950, the term "information retrieval" was
coined by Mooers (1950).

4.2.1 Ranking in Information Retrieval

Information retrieval covers the retrieval process as well as ranking
approaches. The retrieval task is to separate a set of information objects into two subsets; one subset containing the information objects
that meet specific criteria and one subset containing the other documents. Usually, the information objects form a set of documents
that is separated into one subset that contains a search term—the
retrieved documents—and another subset that does not.

Ranking is a function which associates a real number with a document representation in such a way that an ordering among the docu-

ments can be established. The ranking function is designed with the goal that the documents appearing at the top of the ordering are considered to be more likely to be relevant (Baeza-Yates & Ribeiro-Neto, 2003). Even though the retrieval and the ranking process can be differentiated, in information retrieval it is common practice to speak of "retrieval" when "retrieval and ranking" is meant. This becomes feasible when we think about the ranking process as the retrieval of the n documents that have the highest rank. The retrieval process as well as the ranking approach can be either query-dependent or query-independent.

A query-dependent ranking of documents is a ranking function $R_d(q_i, d_j)$ which associates a real number with a query $q_i \in Q$ and a document representation $d_j \in D$. This ranking defines an ordering among the documents with regards to the query q_i (Baeza-Yates & Ribeiro-Neto, 2003). As a matter of course, query-dependent approaches require the entry of a query by the user.

Query-dependent retrieval is traditionally based on term frequencies (Goker & Davies, 2009). The basic assumption is that the more two representations agree in given elements and their distribution, the higher is the probability that they represent similar information. To measure the similarity between documents and queries, those are transferred to a vector representation that allows to apply vector space theory to documents. In the vector space model, the document d is transferred to a vector $\vec{d} = (d_1, d_2, \ldots, d_m)$ of which each component $d_k (1 \leq k \leq m)$ is associated with an index term or predefined keywords. Similarly the query q is expressed as a vector $\vec{q} = (q_1, q_2, \ldots, q_m)$ where the elements $q_k (1 \leq k \leq m)$ are associated with the same terms as the document. The vector can then have binary components expressing whether a term occurs in a document or query. For a more general representation natural numbers can be used to encode the frequency of a term. A document's vector then consists of the number of occurrences of the keywords in the document's text. Furthermore, real numbers are used when terms are weighted according to their importance. The representations of the document and the query are now considered as vectors in a high-dimensional Euclidean space, where each term is assigned a separate dimension (Salton & McGill, 1986). The similarity measure is the cosine of the angle that separates the two vectors of the document and the query (Goker & Davies, 2009). This is also referred to as **cosine similarity** (Ferber, 2003). Generally speaking, modeling documents as vectors is a well established concept in information retrieval (Kao & Poteet, 2010, 2005; Grossman & Frieder, 2004). Even though this traditional approach is sufficient neither for Web pages nor for user-generated content, the vector space model where documents are represented as vectors is a powerful approach. It is a basic concept for the modeling approach introduced in Chapter 5.

Query-independent approaches use other criteria than search terms to retrieve or rank a set of documents. An example for query-independent retrieval is the creation of a subset of documents that are shorter than 125 characters. An example for query-independent ranking is when documents that contain more characters are ranked higher than documents containing less characters. Query-independent ranking can be applied alone or in combination with query-dependent retrieval. Query-independent ranking can also be combined with query-dependent ranking. In this case it serves as improvement of the retrieval process. Query-independent ranking allows to assign scores to documents without the need of a search query entered by the user. This can be useful when search terms are not suitable to represent an information need.

Standard measures of retrieval effectiveness are precision and recall (Saracevic, 2007). **Recall** refers to the attempt to retrieve all the relevant documents and expresses how many of all the relevant documents are retrieved. **Precision** refers to the desire to retrieve as few of the nonrelevant as possible at the same time (Van Rijsbergen, 1979). It provides an indication of the quality of the retrieved document set. Hence, precision is the ratio of the total number of relevant documents retrieved to the total number of documents retrieved. Recall is the ratio of the number of relevant documents retrieved to the total number of documents in the collection (Grossman & Frieder, 2004). In an ideal, perfect retrieval process the set of documents retrieved and the set of relevant documents would be equal. Figure 4.1 illustrates the relationship between precision and recall. Aim of any retrieval process is to retrieve as many relevant documents as possible while minimizing the retrieval of nonrelevant documents.

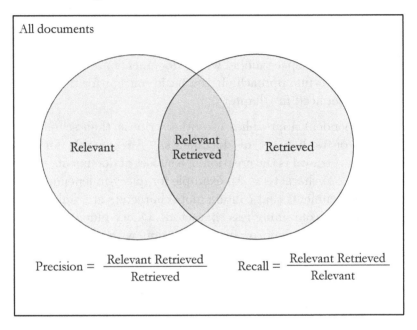

Figure 4.1: Precision and recall.
The result set of a retrieval process comprises documents that are relevant but not retrieved, documents that are retrieved but not relevant and the document that are retrieved and relevant. Precision is the ratio of the correctly retrieved documents and all retrieved documents. Recall is the ratio of the correctly retrieved documents and the total number of relevant documents. Figure adapted from (Grossman & Frieder, 2004).

In the context of this work, the goal is to rank in such a way that as many relevant user-generated content units as possible are ranked highly, while the amount of nonrelevant user-generated content units with a high rank should be minimized.

In information retrieval **relevance** is often described as the correspondence in context between an information requirement statement (a query) and an article (a document) (Salton & McGill, 1986; Ferber, 2003; Saracevic, 2007). This is meant to reflect the degree in which a document satisfies the interest of the user (Saracevic, 2007). A weakness of this notion is that what "satisfies the interest of the user" is hard to grasp. A common practice to seize this notion of relevance is to let "specialists" provide a collection of relevant documents to evaluate the retrieval performance (Baeza-Yates & Ribeiro-Neto, 2003, p. 74). Another serious weakness of this notion is that it does not cover query-independent aspects of relevance. This view does not take into account that there are relevance aspects independent from context and queries. They simply aim at the degree in which the text meets search criteria. To cope with this weakness several models have been developed to describe relevance more specifically. There are two different classes of relevance measures: universal and individual relevance measures, also known as objective and subjective aspects.

The focus of this work is on query-independent ranking based on objective relevance aspects. Query-dependent retrieval can be combined with the approach presented in Chapter 5, but it is not part of this work.

The focus of information retrieval is on query-dependent retrieval and ranking (Li, 2011; Ferber, 2003; Salton & McGill, 1986). Those are well studied whereas query-independent ranking has not been studied as rigorously (Goker & Davies, 2009).

Summing it up, information need and search strategy are user related, whereas the information retrieval method is system related. In a given situation, the information need and the retrieval method are fixed. If information need and retrieval strategy are not appropriate for each other, the only variable the user can alter in the situation is his search

strategy. But, the user can adjust his search strategy only as much as
he system enables it. Table 4.1 shows an overview of the ranges there
are in information need, search strategy and information retrieval
method.

Table 4.1: Overview of user's information needs, search strategies, and
information retrieval methods that can be implemented in a
retrieval system.

	Ranges from...	to...
Information need:	content-related	feature-related
Search strategy:	exploratory	nonexploratory
Information retrieval method:	query-dependent	query-independent

4.2.2 Query-Independent Ranking for Web Page Retrieval

Traditional relevance ranking technologies attempt to retrieve pages
that contain relevant text. But, ranking based on term frequencies
is not strong enough for Web content (Goker & Davies, 2009). An
example scenario shall illustrate that. A user looks for information
about the Canadian government. She formulates the query *Canada
government*. A good result could be any page about important aspects of the topic. Anyhow, a page such as `www.canada.gc.ca` is
likely to be a good answer. Now, let us consider a traditional ranking
process based on term frequencies that aims at getting this page on
top of the ranking in a set that contains 100 million matching pages.
The page has a term frequency of Canada=11 and government=9.[1]
This approach is not strong enough to guarantee a top ranking for
that page. Other pages may contain more occurrences of the query
terms. The two most important sources of information improving the
ranking of Web pages are link structure and URL hierarchy. With

---

[1]Term frequencies are taken from `www.canada.gc.ca`, July 23rd, 2013

3,820 incoming links the page www.canada.gc.ca is relatively heavily linked.[2] Additionally, the URL of this page is a short URL and it is the root page for a hostname. The incoming links might also contain the search terms in their anchor text. The page would be more likely to be on top of a ranking that takes this additional evidence into account. To be useful on Web content query-dependent relevance scores need to be combined with query-independent evidence (Goker & Davies, 2009).

Query-independent ranking is mostly discussed in the context of Web page retrieval (Richardson, Prakash & Brill, 2006). In the context of Web page retrieval query-dependent approaches are also referred to as **dynamic ranking**. Objective relevance is covered by **static ranking**. In Web page retrieval the retrieved and ranked objects are Web pages and the query-independent feature for ranking is based on link analysis. An important approach for the query-independent ranking of Web pages is the PageRank.

Generally speaking, in the first phase of Web retrieval each page is assigned a static rank which is independent of a query. This can be viewed as reflecting the general quality, authority or popularity of a page. It should correspond to a page's or document's prior probability of relevance. The higher the probability of relevance, the higher the static rank. Query matching takes place in the second phase of Web retrieval (Büttcher, Clarke & Cormack, 2010). Since the goal of this work is a query-independent ranking, the focus is on the first phase here.

The PageRank uses incoming links to determine a score for Web pages with respect to its relevance, independent of the user's query (Grossman & Frieder, 2004). The first step and essence of the PageRank is a query-independent ranking algorithm. The PageRank algorithm was introduced by Page et al. in the context of a doctoral thesis at Stanford University supervised by Winograd (Stanford, 2013). Page et al. (1998, p. 1) felt they had to cope with a huge and growing amount of

---

[2]The number of in-linking pages are taken from www.google.com, July 23rd, 2013

diverse data: "Current estimates are that there are over 150 million
Web pages with a doubling life of less than one year. More import-
antly, the Web pages are extremely diverse." Even though diverse in
regards to content, Web pages have a structural feature in common.
They contain additional information in the form of links. Inspired
by academic citation analysis, the PageRank takes advantage of the
link structure of the World Wide Web to produce a global ranking
of Web pages regardless of their content. A Web page is weighed by
the number of other Web pages that link to it. That is the basic
idea. Additionally, the in-linking pages are weighed by the number
of pages that link to them. The result is a recursive algorithm that
ranks Web pages according to importance depending on their connectedness within the link structure of the World Wide Web. The
underlying assumption is that highly linked pages are more important than pages with only a few other pages referencing them. A page
that has many pages linking to it can be just as important as a page
that has only few but highly connected pages linking to it. The idea
of the PageRank can be formalized as follows (Page et al., 1998, p. 3):
u being a Web page, F_u being the set of pages u points to and B_u
being the set of pages that point to u. Let $N_u = |F_u|$ be the number
of forward links from u and let c be a factor for normalization, the
simplified PageRank R is:

$$R(u) = c \sum_{v \in B_u} \frac{R(v)}{N_v} \qquad (4.1)$$

Even though it is efficient for ranking Web pages, the PageRank is
not effective for user-generated content. User-generated content is
part of a Web page. The rank for a Web page is the same for all
user-generated content units on that Web page. The statement that
could be derived from the PageRank for the single user-generated
content unit is meaningless. The granularity of the PageRank is too
coarse for the purpose of ranking user-generated content. Also, the
principle of link analysis is not sufficient for user-generated content.
Commonly, user-generated content units do not contain links. They

do occasionally, but not in an extend that would make link analysis appropriate as ranking feature.

4.3 Shortcomings of Traditional Information Retrieval Concepts

Information retrieval has a relatively long tradition regarding the retrieval of text documents. A feasible question could be if it does deliver approaches that could be applied to user-generated content as well. User-generated content units often contain text as well. They could therefore be treated like other text documents. But, traditional information retrieval focuses on the information the user sends with the search query. The rich source of valuable information that is now available as metadata of user-generated content is not used. Traditional query-dependent approaches can be applied to user-generated content as well, but they do not suffice since they neglect all of the other information a user could use to classify user-generated content.

The large amount of information available online also requires different strategies. Traditional relevance ranking technologies attempt to retrieve pages that contain relevant text. But, ranking based on term frequencies is not strong enough for Web content. The result set of a retrieval process of Web content based on term frequencies can still be very large. Additional information is required to provide users with an appropriate amount of results. To be useful for Web content, query-dependent relevance scores need to be combined with query-independent evidence (Goker & Davies, 2009).

More specialized approaches for Web page retrieval do solve that problem for Web pages, but do not apply to user-generated content either, since the object of retrieval is of a different kind. User-generated content is part of a Web page and not a small Web page for itself. On one Web page there can be many social media entries, all different in quality, authorship, date and relevance. The concept of rating a

Web page is not applicable to social media content. It requires the ranking and rating of content units. That requires a different level of granularity. So, query-independent approaches that are based on link analysis cannot be transferred to user-generated content.

Furthermore, the user's information needs can be different in the context of user-generated content. Of course, a user might also still have content-related information needs concerning user-generated content. He might want to have specific advises others give on, for example, *the successful grow of roses*, expressing *roses* in his search query. But additionally, users might have information needs independent of the content, not expressible in a search query. For example, they want to know which video everybody watches this week. If a user does not know the currently trending video is called *Gangnam Style*, she cannot search for it. Feature-related information needs and query-independent ranking have not been studied as rigorously as query-dependent ranking for content-related search (Goker & Davies, 2009).

Specifically for user-generated content there is a need for research and new approaches especially for query-independent ranking.

5 A Cross-Platform Ranking Approach

The development of a query-independent ranking approach for user-generated content is the main goal of this thesis. The following chapter presents a modeling and a ranking solution[1] based on the insights presented in the previous chapters. Section 5.1 proposes a vector notation for the central characteristics of a user-generated content unit based on the social media document view introduced in Chapter 3.4. The calculation of a ranking that is applicable to all types of user-generated content is proposed in Section 5.2. The example calculation in Chapter 5.3 illustrates the application of the proposed ranking approach by means of user-generated content units from different social media categories.

5.1 Five Scores Reflecting the Social Media Document View

Looking for a solution that solves both, allowing to include more information than what is common for all user-generated content units (i.e., *publishing date*, *author*, and *source*), while maintaining comparability, approaches from other disciplines were evaluated. Encapsulation and information hiding are concepts known from object-oriented software construction (Meyer, 1997). Those are the two fundamental aspects of abstraction in software engineering. Abstraction is the

---

[1] Patent pending.

process of identifying the essential aspects of an entity while ignoring unimportant details. Encapsulation describes a construction that facilitates the bundling of data. The concept of information hiding means that external aspects of an object are separated from its internal details. These concepts simplify the construction and maintenance of software with the help of modularization. An object is a black box that can be constructed and modified independently (Connolly & Begg, 2005, p. 814).

These generic concepts shall serve as inspiration to solve the problem at hand. The measures from different social media platforms differ in specification and target set of a function. Nevertheless, they hold important information that allows to be more precise about the document they belong to.

A user-generated document can be represented as a vector of its properties. The vector notation has been chosen because it is a compact notation suitable for further numerical processing. Let $D = \{d_1, \ldots, d_m\}$ be a set of social media documents and $P(d_i) = (p_1(d_i), \ldots, p_n(d_i))$ be the vector of properties for d_i.

To compare different measures from different categories, one possible solution could be to find correspondent measures throughout the categories. One major drawback of this approach is that there are a lot of measures that do not have correspondents throughout all other categories. Thus, this solution cannot include all information available for all platforms. Furthermore, it involves thorough understanding of platforms to map correspondent measures. Moreover, this has to be done manually. Consequently, this approach does not allow to flexibly and quickly add new platforms.

Another solution is to develop a number of abstract concepts that unite several per se incomparable measures into one aggregated measure, which then allows comparison. Abstraction levels should have semantic correspondents and be category-independent. Different features from different categories are combined in a way that they express the same fact for each category. After normalization of the

co-domains, different aspects become comparable throughout all social media categories. The abstraction levels are individually composed modules, but the modeled aspects are comparable between
social media categories. The result is a vector

$$R(d_i) = (r_1(d_i), \ldots, r'_a(d_i)) \qquad (5.1)$$

where $a \leq n$ and a is constant. $R(d_i)$ holds a fixed number of properties r_j of the social media document d_i. The $r_j(d_i)$ are derived from
one or more properties $p_i(d_i)$.

The social media cross-category comparison shows that there are a
few measures that occur in every category. Namely those are *publishing date, author*, and *source*. All other features are specific for
a certain category or platform (e.g., number of *retweets*). For some
features and categories semantic analogues can be found. *Followers*
in a microblogging service like Twitter are very similar to the *being
in the circles of* that can be found in some social networks.

The number of properties depends on the number of measures that
can be retrieved for a social media document. The number of measures that can be retrieved depends on the measures a platform offers
and in some cases (e.g., author-related information) on the information provided by the user of the platform. Hence, the dimension n of
the property vector $P(d_i) = (p_1(d_i), \ldots, p_n(d_i))$ differs.

To identify a fixed number of abstract concepts that have semantic
correspondents throughout all categories, the measures collected in
Section 3.1 need to be examined for similarities. This has been done
in Section 3.2. The resulting social media document view holds the
common ground for user-generated content of all types.

The identified elements of the social media document view each serve
as the semantic layer of abstract concepts that unite several per se
incomparable measures each into one aggregated measure which then
allows comparison.

The identified elements of the social media document view are:

- author-related information,

- source-related information,

- intrinsic information and

- extrinsic information.

The publishing date belongs to the extrinsic information of a document and is also available for all user-generated content units.

Let $D = \{d_1, \ldots, d_m\}$ be a set of user-generated content units and $P(d_i) = (p_1(d_i), \ldots, p_n(d_i))$ be the properties for d_i.
The properties $P(d_i) = (p_1(d_i), \ldots, p_n(d_i))$ hold the following:
$p_1(d_i), \ldots, p_{h-1}(d_i)$ are all author related measures of d_i,
$p_h(d_i), \ldots, p_{k-1}(d_i)$ are all source related measures of d_i,
$p_k(d_i), \ldots, p_{m-1}(d_i)$ are all intrinsic measures of d_i,
$p_m(d_i), \ldots, p_{n-1}(d_i)$ are all extrinsic measures of d_i, and
$p_n(d_i)$ is the publishing date of d_i.

Now we can derive a vector $R(d_i) = (r_1(d_i), \ldots, r_5(d_i))$ that holds a fixed number of properties of the social media document d_i with the following dimensions:

$$
\begin{pmatrix} r_1(d_i) \\ \ldots \\ r_5(d_i) \end{pmatrix} = \begin{pmatrix} r_{author}(d_i) \\ r_{source}(d_i) \\ r_{intrinsic}(d_i) \\ r_{extrinsic}(d_i) \\ r_{recency}(d_i) \end{pmatrix}
\tag{5.2}
$$

$R(d_i)$ is the **social media document vector**. $r_1, \ldots, r_5$ being abstract concepts of the user-generated content unit d_i.

The five abstract concepts $r_j(d_i)$ are derived from one or more concrete document properties $p_j(d_i)$ and are referred to as follows:
$r_{author}(d_i)$ is derived from $p_1(d_i), \ldots, p_{h-1}(d_i)$,
$r_{source}(d_i)$ is derived from $p_h(d_i), \ldots, p_{k-1}(d_i)$,
$r_{intrinsic}(d_i)$ is derived from $p_k(d_i), \ldots, p_{m-1}(d_i)$,

$r_{extrinsic}(d_i)$ is derived from $p_m(d_i), \ldots, p_{n-1}(d_i)$, and $r_{recency}(d_i)$ is derived from the time of search or processing time and the publishing date $p_n(d_i)$.

Figure 5.1 shows how the proposed social media document view relates to the derived social media document vector that holds a fixed number of properties of the social media document d_i.

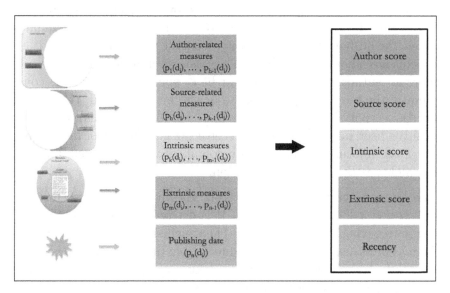

Figure 5.1: From the social media document view to the social media document vector.
The social media document vector comprises five scores. The author score is derived from author-related measures, the source-score is based on source-related measures, intrinsic measures constitute the intrinsic document score, extrinsic measures are the basis for the extrinsic score and recency is derived from the publishing date.

Each score belongs to a document and can be mapped to one single value, the ranking is based on. At the same time it is possible to maintain the scores separate in order to be able to easily adjust the weight of the scores. With regards to the code of conduct no. 3, the

levels of abstraction are modeled in a way that they are comprehens-
ible for the user. This way it is possible to provide the user with an
interface that allows him to factorize different dimensions according
to his needs. The framework proposed here also allows to include or
exclude properties and adjust the way they contribute to the ranking,
if desired.

The **author score** $r_{author}(d_i)$ adapts known concepts described in
Subsection 3.3.1 for social media. It is composed by all metadata
about the author of a user-generated content unit that allow to draw
conclusions about the author. The basic assumptions are that the
more an author is cited, the longer he or she is member of the community, the more contributions he or she has published, the higher
his connectivity in the community (e.g., *number of friends*), the more
positive peer ratings an author received (e.g., *number of likes*), and
the more information the author voluntarily reveals about himself,
the higher is the author's reputation.

The **source score** $r_{source}(d_i)$ adapts known concepts described in
Subsection 3.3.2 for social media. It is derived from metadata about
the source where d_i is published. The conclusions that can be drawn
from a social media source are deduced from the information that can
be assessed about a source. The size of a community can be measured by the *number of members*. The size of a community indicates
the potential reach of a user-generated content unit. For example, a
message being shared through Twitter—a platform that has 200 million active users (Wickre, 2013)—has a higher potential reach than
a message published in a small forum that has 5,000 members. The
number of incoming links is an indicator of the popularity of a source.
This measure is also used as central element of the PageRank (Page
et al., 1998). Hence, the size of the source and number of references
to it will be rewarded.

The **intrinsic score** $r_{intrinsic}(d_i)$ allows to include content-derived
features into the ranking. Several conclusions about the content can
be conducted from consuming the content itself. The properties, that

can be gained by a computer analysis, are limited compared to human capabilities. User-generated content can consist of texts, pictures, video and audio files or a mixture of them. Often, also nontext multimedia content is accompanied by descriptive text. Content-derived features for audio and video content is left to further research. If the content is or contains text, indicators can be gained by text analysis. Text mining is a lively field of research that offers many approaches of different levels of sophistication. Generally, the framework proposed here is open to several solutions. With respect to the desired language-independence, the features proposed here are language-independent. If the approach presented here is applied to content written in a single language only, a more sophisticated language-dependent approach could also be applied. The following are proposals for features that can be easily derived from texts.

The proposed features are meant to be a starting point that can be extended and further developed to more sophisticated levels. The modularity of the proposed framework also allows to neglect single scores such as the intrinsic score of social media documents completely. From studies presented in Subsection 3.3.3, it can be concluded that references contribute to text credibility. Consequently, references will be awarded. Furthermore, text length has shown to be an efficient indicator for text quality. The number of sentences, the number of words per sentence and the number of questions can also be used as features.

The **extrinsic score** $r_{extrinsic}(d_i)$ captures the assessments of user-generated content units described in Subsection 3.3.4. A social media document is part of a lively dynamic system, driven by interactions between users and content, enabled through social media platforms as *recommendations, shares, likes,* and so on. Every interaction with a user-generated content unit contains information about its potential relevance for users that have already consumed a piece of content. That allows to predict the relative probability that a piece of content will be interesting for others. The concept of the extrinsic score is the advancement of the traditional word-of-mouth concept combined with the wisdom of the crowds concept. The collection of all user interactions with a content unit —whether something is read, commented, recommended, shared or liked—is a crowd sourced assessment of the content unit that can serve as recommendation for other users. The extrinsic score is derived from the additional information available on document level. Most of these features are produced by implicit or explicit peer evaluation. Explicit peer evaluations are one click ratings such as *likes* on Facebook, *+1* on Google+, or *thumbs up* on Youtube. *Shares* on Facebook and Twitter are also a kind of explicit peer evaluation. Comments are also a kind of peer evaluation. In the content of the comment users explicitly express their opinion, but implicitly with each comment users show that the content unit was worth spending the time to write the comment. So, whether an explicitly expressed opinion is positive or negative, implicitly every comment shows that the content that is commented on is somehow important. Consequently, the *number of comments* is also a feature indicating relevance. In forums, it is *number of hits* and the size of a thread by *number of replies* to a root-posting that indicate the relevance of a topic and a root posting. In blogs, the *number of comments* per entry shows how much attention a social media document received. The number of links to a blog post, also referred to as track-backs, reveals how often a blog post has been shared and thus recommended. Nowadays, blogs often integrate other social media platforms as plug-ins. Consequently, there can be Facebook *likes*, *+1s*, and other peer ratings also for blog posts. Those are indicators for relevance as well and are integrated into the extrinsic score. In microblogs such as Twitter the same mechanisms can be found. If a social tweet is recommended, it is counted as *retweet* and if it is liked, it is counted as *favorite*.

Recency is a well-known concept for the user. It is the time that has passed between the publication of a piece of content and its consumption by a user. The less time has passed, the more recent is the user-generated content unit. Even though a lot of user-generated content units are time-dependent and more relevant if they are new, this can not be generalized. Consequently, I propose to reward newer content units and to allow the user to adapt recency according to his needs.

5.2 Cross-Platform Compatibility Creates Comparability

To start the calculation of the relevance score, we begin with a set of documents. It is assumed that the documents have been crawled and stored into a database. All dates have already been converted into the same format (e.g., dd-tt-yyyy). Text quality measures have been extracted from the text. Semantically corresponding properties have the same key reference, also referred to as label. For example, *publishing date* is always referenced as *publishing date*, and not sometimes as *date of publication* and other times as *date*. This can be done either on a basic level or it can contain a semantic mapping. For example, *hits* can be mapped to *views*, if desired.

$P(d_i)$ is a map that holds the n properties $p_j, j = 1 \ldots n$ of document d_i as tuples of key and value $(key_j(d_i), value_j(d_i)), j = 1 \ldots n$:
$(key_1(d_i), value_1(d_i)), \ldots, (key_{h-1}(d_i), value_{h-1}(d_i))$: author-related information,
$(key_h(d_i), value_h(d_i)), \ldots, (key_{k-1}(d_i), value_{k-1}(d_i))$: source-related information,
$(key_k(d_i), value_k(d_i)), \ldots, (key_{m-1}(d_i), value_{m-1}(d_i))$: intrinsic information,
$(key_m(d_i), value_m(d_i)), \ldots, (key_{n-1}(d_i), value_{n-1}(d_i))$: extrinsic information, and
$(key_n(d_i), value_n(d_i))$: publishing date.

Each field holds a record with the type of information as key and the value (e.g., key=*hometown*, value=*Vancouver*).

Step 1: Preprocessing

Each property map originally holds information of different types. Such are numeric values such as *hits=100* as well as strings such as *hometown=Vancouver*. The first step maps the nonnumerical information to numerical values. There are several possible solutions how this can be achieved. Finding the best way is a trade-of between information quality and processing efficiency. This question should be evaluated separately, and is not part of this thesis. In the following, one possible solution is introduced.

Studies suggest that the more information an author reveals about himself, the more trustworthy he is regarded (Fogg & Tseng, 1999; Fogg et al., 2000, 2001, 2003; Tseng & Fogg, 1999). Hence, I propose to approximate the users assessment by mapping nonnumerical author related properties such as *age, hometown, hobbies, job*, and so on, to one numerical value as *number of further information given*. This can be achieved by summing the additional information given as a weighted or nonweighted sum, without taking its value into account. On the one hand, a disadvantage of this approach is that it does not take into account if the further information given has any reference to the context of the content the author produced. For example, if a social media document is posted within a forum with a medical focus topic it might make a difference to the reader, if the author claims he is a physician or an undertaker. The approach does not make this distinction. On the other hand, the advantage of the approach is that it is flexible and easily transferable to the variety of author profiles of the different social media platforms. Also, topic identification as well as the mapping of the correspondences between the identified topic and the author information given is not a trivial task. Furthermore, the proposed approach needs less processing time.

Source related properties do not contain nonnumerical properties. Intrinsic and extrinsic properties are available as numerical values as well. Recency is derived from the publishing date.

Step 2: Normalization

For each key the value is normalized with respect to the known maximum. To do that, a comparison map CM is created that holds all keys and their maxima. Each new document is then compared with CM. If a new document holds a property that is not part of CM, CM is updated and the new property is added along with its value as first maximum. If the key is already part of the map, its value is looked up and compared with the new value. If the new value is higher than the prevalent value in CM, the value is reassigned to the key. Next, all the values of the document are normalized with respect to CM. The normalization is based on the achieved maximum of each property. This means that each property is measured in terms of its performance with respect to the global range of this property. This relates the values of the properties of a single user-generated content unit to the values of the properties of other content units. Alternatively, values could be normalized by the average value instead of the maximum value. The average has to be calculated whereas the maximum can be gained by just comparing a new value to the current maximum. Hence, using the maximum is more efficient.

---

initialize empty map CM ;
for *all documents d_i, i=1:m* **do**
    for *all properties p_j, j=1:n of d_i* **do**
        if CM *contains* $key_j(d_i)$ **then**
            if $value(CM.key_j) < value_j(d_i)$ **then**
                set $value(CM.key_j) = value_j(d_i)$
            end
        else
            add p_j to CM
        end
    end
end
for *all documents d_i, i=1:m* **do**
    create empty $P'(d_i)$ that will hold the normalized values for d_i;
    for *all properties p_j, j=1:n of d_i* **do**
        set $key'_j(d_i) = key_j(d_i)$;
        set $value'_j(d_i) = value(key_j(d_i)) \div value(CM.key_j)$
    end
end

Step 3: Aggregation

For each document a new array is created that holds the five document scores. The aggregation is based on the average performance of the properties.

---

for *all documents i=1:m* **do**
    for *all properties p_j, j=1:h-1 of d_i* **do**
    | calculate the average of author related properties $p_j(d_i)$
    end
    for *all properties p_j, j=h:k-1 of d_i* **do**
    | calculate the average of source related properties $p_j(d_i)$
    end
    for *all properties p_j, j=k:m-1 of d_i* **do**
    | calculate the average of intrinsic properties $p_j(d_i)$
    end
    for *all properties p_j, j=m:n-1 of d_i* **do**
    | calculate the average of extrinsic properties $p_j(d_i)$
    end
    for *j=n* **do**
    | calculate recency by the reciprocal of the time difference
    | between publishing time of d_i and processing time
    end
end

Step 4: Reduction to one score

For each document the five scores can now be mapped to one score. A simple approach is to calculate the length of the vector weighing all five scores equally. Alternatively, the euclidean norm could be used, which requires fewer resources for its calculation.

Separability of the Dataset to be Ranked and the Normalization

The proposed approach can be applied to large sets of user-generated content as well as to small subsets. The values for the map CM that are used to normalize measures are proposed to be gathered from the set of content units for which the scores are calculated. Alternatively, the values in map CM used to normalize measures can also be gathered from a different, larger set than the set for which the scores are calculated. For example, if resources are limited, the set of user-generated content units that are ranked can be limited but still be measured in relation to values gained from a larger set of content units. The map CM could even contain manually researched maximum values.

5.3 An Example Case for Forums and Media Sharing Platforms

The following example calculation shall illustrate the method described in the previous section for user-generated content units from different social media categories. The content units are randomly selected from three different forums, and two different media sharing sites. The categories were chosen to demonstrate the range of content units and their metadata. The examples chosen differ in type and number of metadata. Furthermore, they differ in the type of content they contain. User-generated content units from forums contain text, whereas user-generated content units from media sharing sites contain photos or videos.

Table 5.1 shows the metadata for user-generated content units from three different forums and two different media sharing platforms. Example number 1 is from `forum.runnersworld.de`,[2] example number 2 is from `www.laufforum.de`,[3] example number 3 is from `www.apfeltalk.de`,[4] and example number 4 is from `www.apfeltalk.de`[5] as well, example number 5 is from `www.flickr.com`,[6] example number 6 is also from `www.flickr.com`,[7] example number 7 is from

---

[2] http://forum.runnersworld.de/forum/trainingsplanung-fuer-marathon/33367-mit-greif-durchs-trainingsjahr.html
[3] http://www.laufforum.de/immer-noch-kein-speed-87509.html
[4] http://www.apfeltalk.de/forum/macbook-pro-15-a-t410209.html
[5] http://www.apfeltalk.de/forum/showthread.php?t=109921
[6] http://www.flickr.com/photos/28252015@N00/3199464411/
[7] http://www.flickr.com/photos/36755776@N07/7780251000/

www.youtube.com,[8] and example number 8 is from www.youtube.com[9] as well.

The first column of Table 5.1 shows the type of metadata referenced by their labels. The subsequent columns show their values in the different examples. The metadata for examples 1–4 differ from the metadata for examples 5–8. For example, the user-generated content units from Flickr and Youtube have # *likes*, whereas the user-generated content units from the forums do not. Intrinsic measures, that give indications about the quality of the content, derived from the content have been introduced for texts only. Intrinsic measures for multi-media content such as photos and videos are left to further research.

Information about back-links have been gathered from Google. There are also alternative sources for back-links (e.g., Alexa[10]).

Some metadata are differently labeled, but have the same meaning. Some metadata do not have the same but similar meanings. Depending on the desired precision, it is suitable to map those to one metadatum. In the example at hand, some metadata have been semantically mapped. Originally, there are *number of replies* for a forum's content unit and *number of comments* for a media sharing platform's content unit. It is a matter of choice whether to interpret them as expressing the same information or to interpret them as expressing different information. If differently labeled metadata are interpreted to have the same meaning, they can be mapped to one label. If differently labeled metadata are interpreted to have different meanings, different labels should be kept. Here, *number of replies* of a forum's content unit and *number of comments* of a media sharing content unit have been both mapped to *number of replies*. Furthermore, *hits* from forums and *views* from media sharing platforms have been both mapped to *hits*. In some cases, it can make

---

[8]http://www.youtube.com/watch?v=5HHnDEnsdno
[9]http://www.youtube.com/watch?v=GEKgYKpEJ3o
[10]http://www.alexa.com/faqs/?p=91

Table 5.1: Metadata for eight user-generated content units from three different forums and two different media sharing platforms, accessed: August 15, 2012.

Example number	1	2	3	4
Source	Runnersworld	Laufforum	Apfeltalk Forum	Apfeltalk Forum
Author-related measures				
author	Chri.S	docleisen	Blesi	Pansenjoe
realname (0/1)	0	0	0	0
member since (dd.mm.yyyy)	19.10.2006	11.09.2011	16.06.2012	15.11.2007
# contributions	4734	29	76	570
# further information given	7	0	0	0
# contact info	1	0	0	0
# contacts	0	0	0	2
Source-related measures				
backlinks to source URL	20	6	49	49
Intrinsic measures				
# references	0	0	0	0
# words	172	461	109	47
Extrinsic measures				
# replies	9,457	13	520	4616
# hits	1,015,523	194	45,149	513,445
backlinks to content URL	1	0	0	0
Recency				
publishing date (dd.mm.yyyy)	27.11.2007	14.08.2012	29.06.2012	23.11.2007

Example number	5	6	7	8
Source	Flickr	Flickr	Youtube	Youtube
Author-related measures				
author	eddienyc	cromwell_schub	MumfordandSo	Beatlemusical
realname (0/1)	0	0	1	0
member since (dd.mm.yyyy)	01.04.2006	15.03.2009	18.06.2008	05.04.2008
# contributions	0	33	24	34
# further information given	0	3	4	2
# contact info	0	0	2	0
# contacts	0	42	88,023	12,168
# author's views			37,901,475	29,805,112
Source-related measures				
backlinks to source URL	6,610	6,610	6,540	6,540
Intrinsic measures				
Extrinsic measures				
# replies	2	16	3,416	8,851
# hits	706	204	3,956,593	7,543,381
# thumbs up	1	37	17,399	28,925
backlinks to content URL	0	0	321	6
Recency				
publishing date (dd.mm.yyyy)	15.01.2009	22.05.2012	19.10.2009	27.02.2009

sense to differentiate between those two. *Hits* usually indicate that
the user-generated content unit has been clicked on, whereas *views*
indicate that the user-generated content unit has been consumed for
at least a short time.

Then, the maxima of all metadata are gathered as described in Section 5.2, page 111. It holds all occurring types of metadata and the
current maximum values as Table 5.2 shows. Dates such as *member
since* and *publishing date* have been mapped to a numerical value. In
the example given, the maximum value for *member since* has been
calculated as difference in days between the oldest membership and
a reference date. Alternatively, it would also be feasible to set a binary value, to differentiate only the new memberships and not new
memberships.

The maximum value for *publishing date* has been calculated as difference in days between the newest publishing date and a reference
date. The retrieval date served as reference date.

Table 5.2 shows the results of the calculation. When new documents
are added, the map of maxima has to be updated regularly. When it
changes, the scores for the content units have to be updated as well.

Then, the values of the metadata are normalized with respect to
the maxima. The recency of a user-generated content unit $r(d_k)$ is
calculated as the smallest difference between a reference date and the
publishing date of the user-generated content units $d_i, i = 1 \ldots .8$ and
the difference between the publishing date of d_k and the reference
date: $r(d_k) = (\min \Delta d_i)/\Delta d_k$. The calculation of recency applied
here has an exemplary character. Other methods to derive a recency
factor from a publishing date can be applied as well. The choice of
the method depends on which distribution for recency is desired and
the resources that are available for calculation. Table 5.3 shows the
results. All numbers are rounded to three digits after the decimal
point.

Then the author score, source score, intrinsic score, extrinsic score,
and recency are calculated. For the missing intrinsic measures for

Table 5.2: Maximum values of the metadata of examples 1–8.

	Maxima
Author-related measures	
realname (0/1)	1
member since (max(Δd_i))	2294
# contributions	4734
# further information given	7
# contact info	2
# contacts	88,023
# author's views	37,901,475
Source-related measures	
backlinks to source URL	6,610
Intrinsic measures	
# references	0
# words	461
Extrinsic measures	
# replies	9,457
# hits	7,543,381
# thumbs up	28,925
backlinks to content URL	321
Recency	
recency (min(Δd_i))	1

videos and photos, the average intrinsic score of examples 1–4 has been assumed and set for examples 5–8. Table 5.4 shows the results.

Finally, the resulting scores are calculated. There are several options to map the five scores to one. The euclidean norm is one option. In the example given, the arithmetic mean is used. Table 5.5 shows the results. The euclidean norm requires the calculation of the square-root of the sum of the square of all five dimensions, whereas the arithmetic mean only requires the calculation of the sum divided by the number of summands. For large data sets, the arithmetic means might be preferable because it requires less complex calculations. The determination of the optimal solution depends on the application and is left to further research.

Table 5.3: Metadata of examples 1–8 normalized with respect to the maximum values.

Example number	1	2	3	4
Source	Runnersworld	Laufforum	Apfeltalk Forum	Apfeltalk Forum
Author-related measures				
realname (0/1)	0.000	0.000	0.000	0.000
member since $(\Delta d_i/(\max(\Delta d_i)))$	0.914	0.146	0.026	0.745
# contributions	1.000	0.006	0.016	0.120
# further information given	1.000	0.000	0.000	0.000
# contact info	0.500	0.000	0.000	0.000
# contacts	0.000	0.000	0.000	0.000
Source-related measures				
backlinks to source URL	0.003	0.001	0.007	0.007
Intrinsic measures				
# references	0.000	0.000	0.000	0.000
# words	0.373	1.000	0.236	0.102
Extrinsic measures				
# replies	1.000	0.001	0.055	0.488
# hits	0.135	0.000	0.006	0.068
backlinks to content URL	0.003	0.000	0.000	0.000
Recency				
recency $((\min(\Delta d_i))/\Delta d_i)$	0.001	1.000	0.022	0.001

Example number	5	6	7	8
Source	Flickr	Flickr	Youtube	Youtube
Author-related measures				
realname (0/1)	0.000	0.000	1.000	0.000
member since $(\Delta d_i/(\max(\Delta d_i)))$	1.000	0.536	0.653	0.684
# contributions	0.000	0.007	0.005	0.007
# further information given	0.000	0.429	0.571	0.286
# contact info	0.000	0.000	1.000	0.000
# contacts	0.000	0.000	1.000	0.138
# author's views			1.000	0.786
Source-related measures				
backlinks to source URL	1.000	1.000	0.989	0.989
Intrinsic measures				
Extrinsic measures				
# replies	0.000	0.002	0.361	0.936
# hits	0.000	0.000	0.525	1.000
# thumbs up	0.000	0.001	0.602	1.000
backlinks to content URL	0.000	0.000	1.000	0.019
Recency				
recency $((\min(\Delta d_i))/\Delta d_i)$	0.001	0.012	0.001	0.001

Table 5.4: The five relevance scores for examples 1–8.

Example number	1	2	3	4
Source	Runnersworld	Laufforum	Apfeltalk Forum	Apfeltalk Forum
Author score	0.569	0.025	0.007	0.144
Source score	0.003	0.001	0.007	0.007
Intrinsic score	0.187	0.500	0.118	0.051
Extrinsic score	0.379	0.000	0.020	0.185
Recency	0.001	1.000	0.022	0.001

Example number	5	6	7	8
Source	Flickr	Flickr	Youtube	Youtube
Author score	0.167	0.162	0.747	0.272
Source score	1.000	1.000	0.989	0.989
Intrinsic score	0.214	0.214	0.214	0.214
Extrinsic score	0.000	0.001	0.622	0.739
Recency	0.001	0.012	0.001	0.001

Table 5.5: Result scores and ranks for examples 1–8.

Example number	1	2	3	4
Source	Runnersworld	Laufforum	Apfeltalk Forum	Apfeltalk Forum
Result	0.228	0.305	0.035	0.078
Rank	6	3	8	7

Example number	5	6	7	8
Source	Flickr	Flickr	Youtube	Youtube
Result	0.276	0.278	0.515	0.443
Rank	5	4	1	2

Figure 5.2 shows screen-shots of the three user-generated content units with the highest scores. The user-generated content unit with the highest score of the eight examples is a video on Youtube by MumfordandSons. MumfordandSons is the band who plays in the video of example 7. It is a relatively popular band and it is the band's own Youtube-account. This is rewarded with the author-related measure *realname*. MumfordandSons has the highest author score. The second ranked is also a video on Youtube. It is a video of the song *Hey Jude* by The Beatles. It has been watched 7,542,870 times. This is reflected in the highest extrinsic score. The user-generated content unit with the third highest score is a thread in a runner's forum. The second highest author score receives a thread in a runner's forum where Chri.S shares his experiences with his training and gives advice to other runners. Chri.S is an experienced runner and an active user of the forum. In six years of membership he wrote 4,734 contributions in the runner's forum. His high author score reflects this. The example case demonstrates how the proposed approach can be applied to user-generated content units from different platforms of different social media categories. It shows the five scoring dimensions and illustrates how they can be evaluated separately or as one aggregated score.

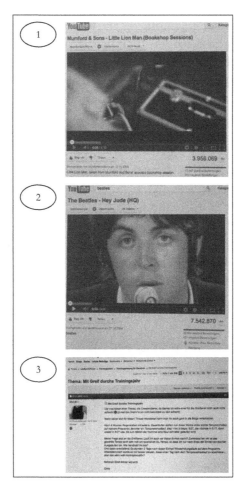

**Figure 5.2: The three user-generated content units of the ex-
ample case with the highest ranks.**
The video on Youtube by Mumford & Sons scored highest of
the eight user-generated content unit in the example. Even
though it has lesser views than the second ranked video the
overall score is higher because of its high author score. The
high author score of the Mumford & Sons video results from
that the video has been posted by the band Mumford &
Sons themselves.

6 Applications

> *Looking at interactive software from a
> radically different, user-centered perspective
> is a necessary step in a rapidly changing
> networked, socially determined information
> world that connects increasing numbers of
> persons in manifold ways.*
>
> Horst Oberquelle (2002, p. 405)

The query-independent ranking method presented in the previous
chapter can be used in a variety of applications. First of all, it can be
applied in a discovery engine for user-generated content. Secondly,
in combination with a query-dependent ranking it can be applied
in a search engine specialized for user-generated content. Thirdly,
the proposed ranking approach can be applied to rank any set of
user-generated content units. For example it could be used to rank
a set of user-generated content units that are part of a social media
monitoring tool. Furthermore, the presented approach can be applied
to all types of documents, for which metadata is available that allows
to determine an author score, a source score, an intrinsic score, an
extrinsic score and a recency score. If information that is required for
one of the scores is missing, the ranking can be based on the remaining
subset of scores. If, for example, there is no information about the
source of a set of documents, the ranking can be based on author-
related information, intrinsic information, extrinsic information, and
recency.

The following chapter presents a concept of a discovery engine for user-generated content in Section 6.1 and a search engine for user-generated content in Section 6.2, as examples for applications of the proposed query-independent ranking approach.

Prior to further processing, content usually needs to be obtained from social media platforms and stored in a database. Figure 6.1 schematically illustrates the main steps.

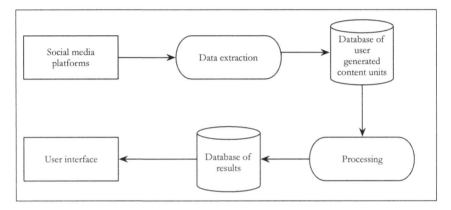

Figure 6.1: Flowchart of how information is obtained from social media platforms for availability in a user interface.
The data extraction process collects user-generated content units and their metadata from social media platforms and stores them in a database. Then, the content units can be processed (e.g., query-independent ranking). The results are stored and can be delivered for display in a user interface.

6.1 A Discovery Engine for User-Generated Content

The proposed ranking approach allows to rank user-generated content units from different platforms independent of a search query. It can be applied in a discovery engine that provides users with the content units that have the highest score of all evaluated content units.

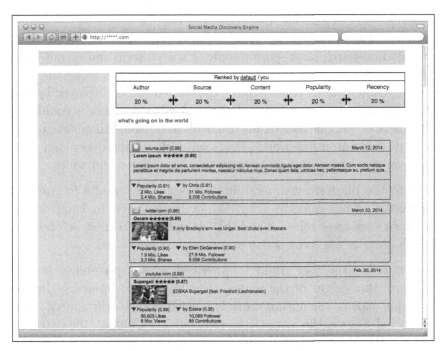

Figure 6.2: A discovery engine for user-generated content is an example application for the proposed query-independent ranking approach.
The main area of the screen shows user-generated content units in the order of their rank. The weight of the five scores can be adjusted by the user according to his interests and information needs.

Figure 6.2 shows a wireframe of the proposed concept. The main area in the center shows user-generated content units from different platforms. The user-generated content units are displayed in the order of their rank based on the five scores. Figure 6.3 specifies in detail the presentation of content units. The more user-generated content units the discovery engine evaluates, the worthier are the results. Ideally, the discovery engine covers all public user-generated content units.

The discovery engine for user-generated content enables exploratory search and is suited for users with feature-related information needs, who do not search for a specific topic or search term and do not have an exact idea of what they want to find. A user who seeks the best scoring content units could explore the content units displayed by the discovery engine in the order of their overall score. Users could use the discovery engine to look for inspiration, for something new, or for *what is going on in the world*. Users can visit the discovery engine to discover what people share, comment on and like world wide.

Due to the platform comparability users get the results for various platforms. Consequently, they do not longer need to know which platforms are most relevant and they do not need to know beforehand which authors are most active and most recommended.

Additionally, the user could be provided with a possibility to manipulate the weight of the scores according to his interests. In the example shown, the author score is labeled *Author*, the source score is labeled *Source*, the intrinsic score is labeled *Content*, the extrinsic score is labeled *Popularity*, and the recency score is labeled *Recency*. The labels have been chosen to indicate the meaning of the scores. For example, if a user is interested in the highest scoring sources, he could set the source score to 100 percent, thus setting all other scores to zero and browse through the results. If he is interested in the most active and most recommended authors, he could set the author score to 100 percent, thus setting all other scores to zero and browse through the results.

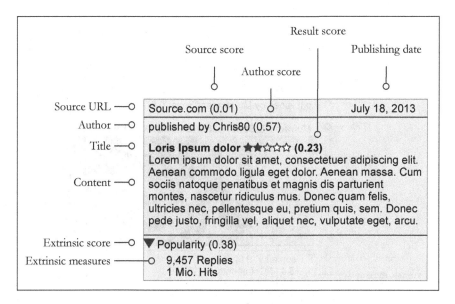

Figure 6.3: Key to ranked user-generated content units.
The content of a content unit is displayed in the central area. At the top, the source URL and its source score is displayed along with the publishing date. Below this, the author and the author score is given. Directly above the content, the title of the contribution is provided. Next to the title the result score is visualized by stars. The result score is also provided in numerical form. At the bottom the extrinsic score is displayed as *popularity*. Below the extrinsic score, the extrinsic measures that led to the extrinsic score are provided. The triangle next to *Popularity* indicates that measures can be displayed or hidden as desired.

The features used in the proposed query-independent ranking approach are all language-independent. It is therefore possible to apply it to content units of different languages. Provided that content units are separable by language,[1] it would also be possible to filter content units by language and to compare results from different languages.

---

[1]For example, content could be tagged during the data extraction process.

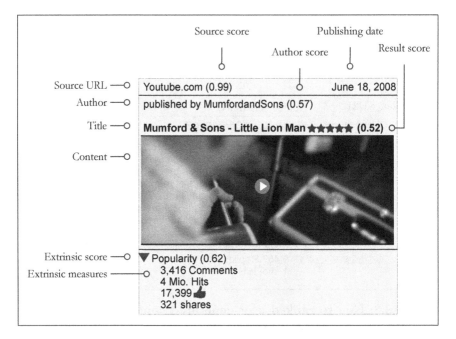

Figure 6.4: Key to ranked user-generated content units using the example of a Youtube video.
The figure shows the visualization of ranked user-generated content units for a concrete video on Youtube. The values of the measures and scores are taken from the example calculation presented in Section 5.3.

The author score, source score, intrinsic score, extrinsic score, and recency are additional information that support the user to orientate himself. It enhances transparency, because all available metadata can be displayed together. The user does not have to search for additional metadata on other pages anymore (as it is usually the case for author related information and source related information). Furthermore, he does not need to rely on a feeling gained from experience to interpret the metadata. Metadata is already normalized in relation to other user-generated content units' values and displayed with the content. Figure 6.3 shows how ranked content units could be displayed in the discovery engine's interface. Figure 6.4 gives an example for a video. This application provides the user with a source of information that is independent of what is shared in his own, limited social environment.

6.2 A Search Engine for User-Generated Content

Today, for many users search engines are their main entrance to the World Wide Web (Hearst, 2009).[2]

Search engines usually welcome their users with a blank page featuring the search field (e.g., Google,[3] Bing,[4] search.com,[5] WolframAlpha[6]). They do not show content before the user has entered a keyword. These search engines allow nonexploratory search for content-related search needs only. The proposed query-independent ranking approach can be used in combination with a query-dependent ranking approach for a search engine for user-generated content that supports exploratory as well as nonexploratory search.

Figure 6.5 shows a concept of the social media search engine. It allows users to express content-related information needs in addition to feature-related information needs.

The social media search engine illustrated in Figure 6.5 is an extension of the concept presented in the previous section. It is extended by the possibility to search content units by entering a search query in the search field. The main part of the interface is the result area, which displays the user-generated content units with the highest scores.

---

[2]The results of a Web site ranking indicate that this might change in favor of social media applications. The first and the second of the Web sites with the most traffic are `https://www.google.com` and `https://www.facebook.com` by turns (Alexa, 2013). The calculation of traffic is based on a combination of average daily visitors and pageviews over the past month.

[3]`http://www.google.com`

[4]`http://www.bing.com`

[5]`http://www.search.com`

[6]`http://www.wolframalpha.com`

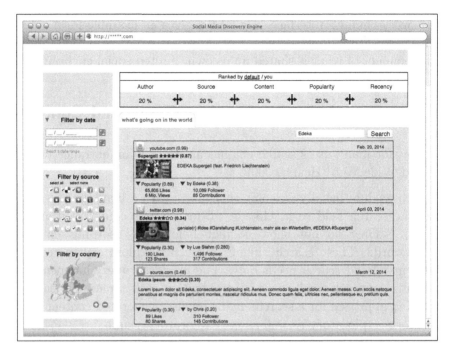

Figure 6.5: A search engine for user-generated content is
an example application for the proposed query-
independent ranking approach.
The main area of the screen shows user-generated content
units, ordered by rank. The user can type in search queries
to filter the user-generated content units with regards to a
specific topic for example. The weight of the five scores can
be adjusted according to the user's interests. Additionally,
the user can filter content by date, by source and by country.

The scores serve as additional information for the user. They help
him to orientate himself and to classify the search results.

Furthermore, additional filter concepts are added. If the information
is available in the database, content units can be filtered by specific
dates, sources, or countries. The left hand side of Figure 6.5 indicates
further possibilities to integrate filter concepts. Alternatively, the

user could be offered the possibility to filter not by source but by social media type.

There are several possibilities to combine query-independent and query-dependent rankings (Craswell et al., 2005). The search query can be used as filter to the ranked lists of user-generated content units. The set of user-generated content units is divided into two subsets: one subset containing the content units in which the entered search query occurs and one subset containing the content units in which the entered search query does not occur.

An improved approach calculates a second query-dependent rank that reflects the degree of correspondence between the text and the search query. Information retrieval offers a variety of approaches for query-dependent ranking of text documents. The query-dependent rank is combined with the query-independent rank.

Not all user-generated content units consist of text only. This can be a problem for text based ranking approaches. Videos and pictures from media sharing platforms for example, usually contain only a few words. The text can be found in the title or the description of the medium. Some platforms allow to tag pictures or videos with descriptive words (e.g., Flickr). Those can be used for the query-dependent ranking of user-generated content units of this type.

7 Conclusion

This final chapter provides a summary of the most important results of this work in Section 7.1 before outlining potentials for further work and research in Section 7.2.

7.1 Summary

This thesis started out with the problem that user-generated content units provide various information in their metadata that could help to evaluate them, but is left unused due to a lack of comparability. Considering the massive amount of user-generated content that is already available and that is continuously produced, users need assistance in their task to find and evaluate user-generated content units to tap the full potential of social media.

This thesis provides a framework to compare entities by different types and number of measures. This is achieved through the identification of appropriate levels to which the measures can be aggregated and that are common for all entities.

Specifically, this thesis provides a query-independent ranking method to compare user-generated content units from different social media platforms with each other. It solves the problem of comparability of metadata of different quantity and types as it is the case for user-generated content. This is done by providing a model that can be applied to user-generated content with different metadata. The approach maps different metadata to aspects that are common for all types of user-generated content.

For each user-generated content unit a score for each aspect is calculated. A user-generated content unit is represented by a vector of its scores. The scores are derived from measures that can be obtained from metadata.

The modeled aspects are: author-related information, source-related information, intrinsic information and extrinsic information and recency. For each aspect the related information is normalized with respect to the maximum known value for the information. It thus relates the information for a given user-generated content unit to other user-generated content units. For a single content unit it helps the user to estimate the magnitude of the numbers provided in its metadata.

The five scores for each document can be mapped to a single score. For a given set of user-generated content units this allows to compare them and establish an order among them. This work also provides a suggestion for an interface and a visualization of the ranked user-generated content units.

The proposed approach is language-independent. Therefore, it can be applied to user-generated content independent of the language of their content.

The proposed query-independent ranking can be combined with query-dependent ranking to built a search engine for user-generated content that accounts for the specific characteristics of user-generated content.

The application of the approach proposed in this thesis helps users to access the value of social media and to unlock more of its potential.

7.2 Extensions and Further Research

This section suggests further research and work from technical details closely related to the approach presented in this thesis to more comprehensive propositions, the latter also addressing challenges beyond the scope of this work.

Further research might explore solutions to derive intrinsic measures from pictures, audio files, and videos. A measure that indicates quality for media files could for example be the file size, assuming that a larger file size indicates a higher resolution. But for online content the file size is often reduced and optimized for fast transfer. Therefore, the file size is not necessarily suitable as quality indicator.

Further work could extend the author score. Let the connections an author has be his primary connections and the connections of his primary connections be his secondary connections. The author score could be extended from taking only first-degree connections into account to including connections of further degrees into the author score. Given that the information is available not only about how many connections an author has, but also who he is connected with, the use of this information might be a reasonable extension for the author score. A solution to integrate this information is, to assign a weight to every primary connection depending on the primary connection's number of primary connections. This way, the number of secondary connections of an author can be included into her author score. This could be continued with a decreasing impact for further degrees of connections. A simplified example for Twitter shall illustrate this mechanism. Twitter-author A has 10 followers which have an average of 10 followers, Twitter-author B has 50 followers which have an average of 10 followers and Twitter-author C has also 50 followers which have an average of 100 followers. We could compare them based on their primary connections by the number of their followers. Then, the author scores of Twitter-author B and Twitter-author C would be equal. But, let us assume we have a 50 percent probability that the people who follow Twitter-author B and C share their tweets. Then, a tweet by author B would reach his 50 followers plus half of the followers of his followers, hence 300 people. A tweet by author C would also reach his 50 followers plus half of the followers of his followers, hence 2,550 people. Consequently, it can be reasoned that, even though author B has the same number of primary connections as author C, author C's tweet will probably reach more people than a tweet from B. The implementation of this approach requires more complex data retrieval and storage than the approach presented in this work. Whether the increased complexity is worth the gain in precision is left to further research.

Further work might also investigate possibilities to extend the proposed approach to collaboratively created content. The proposed model assumes that a user-generated content unit has one author and one publishing date. Collaboratively created content, such as wiki-articles, can be created by many authors. Wiki-articles are also object to continuous changes that are preserved in their editing history. A considerable amount of work has investigated the possibilities to analyze wiki-content and editing history. It would be interesting to explore possibilities to make results from wiki analysis comparable to other types of content as well.

The object of the ranking proposed in this work is the social media document (cf., Section 3.2) that can be allocated to level 1 in Figure 3.13 on page 73 and to level 1 in Figure 7.1. For specific platforms, there is an additional level above these contributions. This is the case for location sharing and annotation platforms as well as rating and review platforms. For location sharing and annotation platforms the ranked objects are the annotations (cf., level 1 in Figure 7.1) of locations (cf., level 0 in Figure 7.1). For rating and review platforms the ranked objects are the reviews, which refer to a product or service. The proposed ranking approach ranks the annotations and reviews (cf., level 1 in Figure 7.1). The object of these contributions—location, product, or service—is allocated on level 0 in Figure 7.1. In contrast to the contributions on level 1, the object of a contribution on level 0 is not a social media document as described in the social media document view in Section 3.4. In the case of location sharing and annotation platforms, the annotations refer to locations. Locations do not have a distinct author and publishing date. In the case of rating and review platforms, ratings and reviews refer to a product or

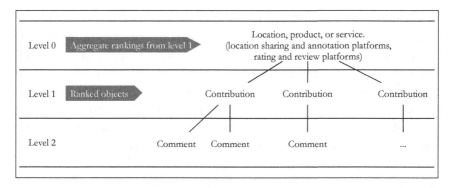

Figure 7.1: Additional aggregation level for locations and products.
Location sharing and annotation platforms as well as rating and review platforms have an additional level of content: level 0. Level 0 comprises locations, products, and services, which are objects of contributions. The contributions on level 1 are the objects of the ranking proposed in this work. Future work could investigate ways to aggregate the ranking of user-generated content units on level 1 to a higher reference point on level 0.

service, which do not have a publishing date or author. Nevertheless, the average rating of a product is an indicator for the quality of the product, service, or experience reviewed. Consequently, for platforms of this type, level 0 is also a relevant level of consideration. Further work could investigate possibilities to aggregate the ranking of user-generated content units to a higher reference point, such as products, services, or venues. For a single source this might be straightforward, but the possibilities of integration into a cross-category compatible framework, as it is proposed in this work, needs to be investigated.

Furthermore, future research could evaluate alternative designs to refine the concepts proposed in Chapter 6 with regard to usability. The work at hand enables to display information to the user that helps him to evaluate user-generated content. On the one hand, this additional information can be a useful guidance. On the other hand, too much information displayed at once could lead to counterproductive complexity of the interface. Chapter 6 provides a suggestion how to display and visualize ranked user-generated content units (cf., Figure 6.3 on page 127 and Figure 6.4 on page 128). Future research could investigate whether all measures and scores should be provided to the user at once or it is more useful to display a subset, that for example could consist of the scores only. Furthermore, it could be evaluated whether it contributes more to usability to display numerical values or to transfer the values into a visualization. The visualization of the values gives rise to the question on which level of detail the visualization should represent the numerical values. Further work might explore how this additional information should be visualized in a way that it is most compressible and contributes most to usability.

Beyond the scope of this thesis, there are adjacent areas that can be further developed to efficiently apply the proposed query-independent ranking approach to large sets of user-generated content. This concerns the data extraction process from the social media platforms and the data base design for example. The amount of user-generated content produced per time unit is enormous and a real-time application with the proposed features is a challenge for which strategies for efficient data processing still need to be developed.

Appendix: Collection of User-Generated Content Metadata

This appendix presents a full collection of metadata available for each of the evaluated categories. All measures are sorted according to the social media document view introduced in Section 3.4. Measures are listed independent of their significance for the ranking of user-generated content units. The following lists represent a collection of the measures generally available.

Measures in Blogs

Blogs
Author-related measures
author id
Source-related measures
backlinks to source URL
Intrinsic measures
references
words
Extrinsic measures
comments, # replies
views
backlinks to content URL (trackbacks)
publishing date (dd.mm.yyyy)
Plug-ins from other platforms
likes (Facebook)
+1 (Google+)
shares (Facebook)
shares (Twitter)
shares (LinkedIn)
shares (Tumblr.com)
pins (Pinterest.com)
flattrs (microdonations, Flattr.com)
stumbles (Stumbleupon.com)

Data accessed: August 15, 2012
Example sources:
www.bildblog.de,
perezhilton.com,
michellemalkin.com,
www.my-diary.org

Measures in Forums

	Forums
Author-related measures	
	author id
	membership since
	# postings
	recency of latest activity
	location
	hometown
	age
	contact information
	number of contacts within the forum's community (if applicable)
Source-related measures	
	# backlinks to source URL
	# (active) memebrs
Intrinsic measures	
	# references
	# words
Extrinsic measures	
	# replies
	# views
	# threads in topic
	# postings in topc
	# recency of newest posting in topic
	# views of thread
	publishing date (dd.mm.yyyy)

Data accessed: August 15, 2012
Example sources:
http://www.gaiaonline.com/forum/ (phpBB)
http://www.ioff.de/ (vBulletin)
https://discussions.apple.com/index.jspa
http://www.apfeltalk.de/forum/content/
http://forum.football.co.uk/
http://forums.bit-tech.net/

Measures in Location Sharing and Annotation Platforms

Location Sharing and Annotation
Author-related measures
author id
real name
friends
mayorships
badges
tips
lists
check-ins
photos
location
about me sentence
Source-related measures
backlinks to source URL
Intrinsic measures
references
words
Extrinsic measures
likes
visitors of location
check-ins of location
likes of location
dislikes of location
mayor of location
number of check-ins in the last n (e.g.,n= 60) days required to become mayor of location
number of pictures of location
tips of location
done bys of tip
highlights of location
publishing date (dd.mm.yyyy)

Data accessed: August 15, 2012
Example sources:
https://foursquare.com/
http://gowalla.com (has been shut down in 2012)

Measures in Media Sharing Platforms

Media Sharing
Author-related measures
author id
real name
membership since
contributions
subscribers
recency of lastest activity
channel views
testimonials
favorites by others
groups
Source-related measures
backlinks to source URL
memebrs
Intrinsic measures
resolution
Extrinsic measures
comments
views
likes
dislikes
favorites
honors
backlinks to content URL (trackbacks)
publishing date (dd.mm.yyyy)

Data accessed: August 15, 2012
Example sources:
http://www.youtube.com/
http://www.flickr.com/

Measures in Microblogs

Microblogs
Author-related measures
author id
real name
tweets
followers
followings
recency of latest tweet
Source-related measures
backlinks to source URL
members
Intrinsic measures
references
words
tags
Extrinsic measures
retweets
favorites
publishing date (dd.mm.yyyy)

Data accessed: August 15, 2012
Example source:
https://twitter.com

Measures in Question and Answer Platforms

Question and Answer Platforms
Author-related measures
author id
membership since
questions
answers
best answers
recency of last contribution
trust points
location
hometown
age
Source-related measures
backlinks to source URL
Intrinsic measures
references
words
Extrinsic measures
answers
stars, likes
publishing date (dd.mm.yyyy)

Data accessed: August 15, 2012
Example sources:
http://wiki.answers.com/
http://answers.yahoo.com/

Measures in Rating and Review Platforms

Rating and Review Platforms
Author-related measures
author id
real name
reviews
of helpful reviews
contact information
Source-related measures
backlinks to source URL
Intrinsic measures
references
words
Extrinsic measures
found the review helpful
comments
stars of reviewed object
reviews for reviewed object
publishing date (dd.mm.yyyy)

Data accessed: August 15, 2012
Example sources:
http://www.amazon.com
http://www.epinions.com
http://www.qype.com
http://www.yelp.co.uk/

Measures in Social Networks

Social Networks
Author-related measures
author id
real name
member since
recency of last contribution
friends, followers
Source-related measures
members
backlinks to source URL
Intrinsic measures
references
words
Extrinsic measures
comments
likes
shares
publishing date (dd.mm.yyyy)

Data accessed: August 15, 2012
Example sources:
https://facebook.com
https://plus.google.com
http://www.xing.com
http://www.linkedin.com

Bibliography

Agichtein, E., Castillo, C., Donato, D., Gionis, A. & Mishne, G. (2008). Finding High-Quality Content in Social Media. In: Proceedings of the International Conference on Web Search and Web Data Mining. WSDM '08, ACM, New York, pp. 183–194.

Ahn, J. & Brusilovsky, P. (2009). Adaptive Visualization of Search Results: Bringing User Models to Visual Analytics. Information Visualization, vol. 8, 3, pp. 167–179.

Alexa (2013). The Top 500 Sites on the Web. URL: http://www.alexa.com/topsites, accessed: September 5, 2013.

Ammann, R. (2009). Jorn Barger, the Newspage Network and the Emergence of the Weblog Community. In: Proceedings of the 20th ACM Conference on Hypertext and Hypermedia. HT '09, ACM, New York, pp. 279–288.

Anderka, M., Stein, B. & Lipka, N. (2011a). Detection of Text Quality Flaws as a One-Class Classification Problem. In: Proceedings of the 20th ACM International Conference on Information and Knowledge Management. CIKM '11, ACM, New York, pp. 2313–2316.

Anderka, M., Stein, B. & Lipka, N. (2011b). Towards Automatic Quality Assurance in Wikipedia. In: Proceedings of the 20th International Conference Companion on World Wide Web, Hyderabad. WWW '11, ACM, New York, pp. 5–6.

Anderson, P. (2012). Web 2.0 and Beyond: Principles and Technologies. Taylor & Francis, Boca Raton, FL, USA.

Archak, N., Ghose, A. & Ipeirotis, P.G. (2007). Show me the Money!

Deriving the Pricing Power of Product Features by Mining Consumer Reviews. In: Proceedings of the 13th ACM SIGKDD International Conference on Knowledge Discovery and Data Mining. KDD '07, ACM, New York, pp. 56–65.

Baeza-Yates, R., Boldi, P., Bozzon, A., Brambilla, M., Ceri, S. & Pasi, G. (2011). Trends in Search Interaction. In: S. Ceri & M. Brambilla (Eds.), Search Computing, Springer-Verlag, Heidelberg. pp. 26–32.

Baeza-Yates, R. & Ribeiro-Neto, B. (2003). Modern Information Retrieval. ACM Press Books, New York.

Barkhuus, L., Brown, B., Bell, M., Sherwood, S., Hall, M. & Chalmers, M. (2008). From Awareness to Repartee: Sharing Location Within Social Groups. In: Proceedings of the SIGCHI Conference on Human Factors in Computing Systems. CHI '08, ACM, Florence, pp. 497–506.

Beadon, L. (2013). Funniest/Most Insightful Comments Of The Week At Techdirt. URL: `http://www.techdirt.com/articles/20130922/09493824615/funniestmost-insightful-comments-week-techdirt.shtml`, accessed: September 23, 2013.

Berners-Lee, T. (1996). WWW: Past, Present, and Future. Computer, vol. 29, 10, pp. 69–77.

Boyd, D. & Ellison, N. (2008). Social Network Sites: Definition, History, and Scholarship. Journal of Computer-Mediated Communication, vol. 13, 1, pp. 210–230.

Bush, V. (1945). As We May Think. Atlantic Monthly, vol. 176, 1, pp. 101–108.

Büttcher, S., Clarke, C. & Cormack, G. (2010). Information Retrieval: Implementing and Evaluating Search Engines. The MIT Press, Cambridge, MA, USA.

CapsuleHD20 (2012). PSY - Gangnam Style (Comeback Stage) - Inkigayo. URL: `http://www.youtube.com/watch?v=6OMQ3AG1c8o`, accessed: September 25, 2013.

Chen, Y. & Xie, J. (2008). Online Consumer Review: Word-of-Mouth as a New Element of Marketing Communication Mix. Management Science, vol. 54, 3, pp. 477–491.

Chen, Y.Y., Liu, C.L., Chang, T.H. & Lee, C.H. (2010). An Unsupervised Automated Essay Scoring System. IEEE Intelligent Systems, vol. 25, pp. 61–67.

Ciao (2013). Erfahrungsberichte. URL: http://www.ciao.de/ Braun_Oral_B_Professional_Care_7000_Black__11152413, accessed: September 26, 2013.

CNN (2009). US Airways Plane Down in Hodson River. URL: http://www.youtube.com/watch?v=b1osGeJwwtQ, accessed: August 12, 2013.

Connolly, T. & Begg, C. (2005). Database Systems: a Practical Approach to Design, Implementation, and Management. Addison-Wesley Longman, Essex.

Cramer, H., Rost, M. & Holmquist, L.E. (2011). Performing a Check-in: Emerging Practices, Norms and 'Conflicts' in Location-Sharing Using Foursquare. In: Proceedings of the 13th International Conference on Human Computer Interaction with Mobile Devices and Services. MobileHCI '11, ACM, New York, pp. 57–66.

Craswell, N., Robertson, S., Zaragoza, H. & Taylor, M. (2005). Relevance Weighting for Query Independent Evidence. In: Proceedings of the 28th Annual International ACM SIGIR Conference on Research and Development in Information Retrieval, Salvador, Brazil. SIGIR '05, ACM, New York, pp. 416–423.

Daer, A. (2013). User Profile. URL: https://foursquare.com/ alicedaer, accessed: September 24, 2013.

Dalip, D.H., Gonçalves, M.A., Cristo, M. & Calado, P. (2009). Automatic Quality Assessment of Content Created Collaboratively by Web Communities: A Case Study of Wikipedia. In: Proceedings of the 9th ACM/IEEE-CS Joint Conference on Digital Libraries,

Austin. JCDL '09, ACM, New York, pp. 295–304.

Diamond, L. (2010). Liberation Technology. Journal of Democracy, vol. 21, 3, pp. 69–83. URL: http://muse.jhu.edu/, accessed: August 13, 2013.

DPA (2010). WeTab-Chef zieht sich zurück. URL: http://www.zeit.de/wirtschaft/unternehmen/2010-10/wetab-chef-rueckzug, accessed: August 15, 2013.

Elgersma, E. & de Rijke, M. (2008). Personal vs Non-Personal Blogs: Initial Classification Experiments. In: Proceedings of the 31st Annual International ACM SIGIR Conference on Research and Development in Information Retrieval, Singapore. SIGIR '08, ACM, New York, pp. 723–724.

Elsas, J.L. & Glance, N. (2010). Shopping for Top Forums: Discovering Online Discussion for Product Research. In: Proceedings of the First Workshop on Social Media Analytics, Washington. SOMA '10, ACM, New York, pp. 23–30.

Encyclopædia Britannica (2007). The New Encyclopædia Britannica Macropædia, vol. 26. Encyclopædia Britannica, Inc., Chicago, 15th ed.

Encyclopædia Britannica (2013a). Broadcasting. URL: http://www.britannica.com/EBchecked/topic/80543/broadcasting, accessed: August 12, 2013.

Encyclopædia Britannica (2013b). Social Network. URL: http://www.britannica.com/EBchecked/topic/1335211/social-network, accessed: August 2nd, 2013.

Encyclopædia Britannica (2013c). World Wide Web (WWW). URL: http://www.britannica.com/EBchecked/topic/649051/World-Wide-Web-WWW, accessed: August 2nd, 2013.

Facebook (2013). Key Facts. URL: http://newsroom.fb.com/Key-Facts, accessed: August 16, 2013.

Ferber, R. (2003). Information Retrieval: Suchmodelle und Data-Mining-Verfahren für Textsammlungen und das Web. dpunkt Verlag, Heidelberg.

Fischer, E. & Reuber, A. (2011). Social Interaction via New Social Media: (How) Can Interactions on Twitter Affect Effectual Thinking and Behavior? Journal of Business Venturing, vol. 26, 1, pp. 1–18.

Fischer, G. (2011). Understanding, Fostering, and Supporting Cultures of Participation. interactions, vol. 18, pp. 42–53.

Fogg, B., Marshall, J., Laraki, O., Osipovich, A., Varma, C., Fang, N., Paul, J., Rangnekar, A., Shon, J., Swani, P. & Treinen, M. (2001). What Makes A Web Site Credible? A Report on a Large Quantitative Study. In: Proceedings of ACM CHI 2001 Conference on Human Factors in Computing Systems, Seattle. ACM, New York, vol. 1, pp. 61–68.

Fogg, B., Marshall, J., Osipovich, A., Varma, C., Laraki, O., Fang, N., Paul, J., Rangnekar, A., Shon, J., Swani, P. et al. (2000). Elements that Affect Web Credibility: Early Results from a Self-Report Study. In: CHI'00 extended abstracts on Human factors in Computing Systems, The Hague. ACM, New York, pp. 287–288.

Fogg, B., Soohoo, C., Danielson, D., Marable, L., Stanford, J. & Tauber, E. (2003). How do Users Evaluate the Credibility of Web Sites? In: Proceedings of the 2003 Conference on Designing for User Experiences, San Francisco. ACM, New York, pp. 1–15.

Fogg, B.J. & Tseng, H. (1999). The Elements of Computer Credibility. In: Proceedings of the SIGCHI Conference on Human Factors in Computing Systems: the CHI is the Limit. CHI '99, ACM, New York, pp. 80–87.

Foster, M., Francescucci, A. & West, B. (2010). Why Users Participate in Online Social Networks. International Journal of E-Business Management, vol. 4, 1, p. 3.

Foursquare (2013). New York Marriott Marquis. URL: `https://foursquare.com/v/new-york-marriott-marquis/` `439c437bf964a520f02b1fe3`, accessed: September 24, 2013.

Garlesteanu, C. (2013). Rusty Scissor. URL: `http://www.flickr.` `com/photos/12240548@N02/9919681903/in/photostream`, accessed: September 25, 2013.

Ghonim, W. (2012). Revolution 2.0: The Power of the People Is Greater Than the People in Power — A Memoir. Houghton Mifflin Harcourt, New York.

Goker, A. & Davies, J. (2009). Information Retrieval: Searching in the 21st Century. John Wiley & Sons Ltd.Wiley, West Sussex, United Kindom.

Grabs, A. & Bannour, K.P. (2011). Follow me! Erfolgreiches Social Media Marketing mit Facebook, Twitter und Co. Galileo Press, Bonn.

Grace, J.H., Zhao, D. & Boyd, D. (2010). Microblogging: What and How Can we Learn from It? In: Proceedings of the 28th of the International Conference Extended Abstracts on Human Factors in Computing Systems, Atlanta. CHI EA '10, ACM, New York, pp. 4517–4520.

Grossman, D. & Frieder, O. (2004). Information Retrieval: Algorithms and Heuristics. Springer, Dordrecht, Netherlands.

Hale, A. & Opondo, M. (2005). Humanising the Cut Flower Chain: Confronting the Realities of Flower Production for Workers in Kenya. Antipode, vol. 37, 2, pp. 301–323.

Hannak, A., Sapiezynski, P., Molavi Kakhki, A., Krishnamurthy, B., Lazer, D., Mislove, A. & Wilson, C. (2013). Measuring Personalization of Web Search. In: Proceedings of the 22nd International Conference on World Wide Web, Rio de Janeiro. International World Wide Web Conferences Steering Committee, Geneva, Switzerland, pp. 527–538.

Hanrahan, J. (2009). I Just Watched a Plane Crash. URL: https://twitter.com/highfours/status/1121908186, accessed: August 12, 2013.

Hansen, D., Shneiderman, B. & Smith, M.A. (2010). Analyzing Social Media Networks with NodeXL: Insights from a Connected World. Morgan Kaufmann, San Francisco.

Harper, R.H.R., Lamming, M.G. & Newman, W.M. (1992). Locating Systems at Work: Implications for the Development of Active Badge Applications. Interacting with Computers, vol. 4, 3, pp. 343–363.

Hearst, M.A. (2009). Search User Interfaces. Cambridge University Press, New York.

Hoffmann, S. & Hutter, K. (2012). Carrotmob as a New Form of Ethical Consumption. The Nature of the Concept and Avenues for Future Research. Journal of Consumer Policy, vol. 35, 2, pp. 215–236.

Hu, M., Lim, E.P., Sun, A., Lauw, H.W. & Vuong, B.Q. (2007). Measuring Article Quality in Wikipedia: Models and Evaluation. In: Proceedings of the 16th ACM Conference on Conference on Information and Knowledge Management, Lisbon. CIKM '07, ACM, New York, pp. 243–252.

Iachello, G., Smith, I., Consolvo, S., Chen, M. & Abowd, G. (2005). Developing Privacy Guidelines for Social Location Disclosure Applications and Services. In: Proceedings of the 2005 Symposium on Usable Privacy and Security, Pittsburgh. ACM, New York, pp. 65–76.

Irving, S., Harrison, R. & Rayner, M. (2002). Ethical Consumerism — Democracy Through The Wallet. Journal of Research for Consumers, vol. 3, 3.

Jansen, B., Zhang, M. & Zhang, Y. (2007). Brand Awareness and the Evaluation of Search Results. In: Proceedings of the 16th

International Conference on World Wide Web, Banff. ACM, New York, pp. 1139–1140.

Kakkonen, T., Myller, N., Timonen, J. & Sutinen, E. (2005). Automatic Essay Grading with Probabilistic Latent Semantic Analysis. In: Proceedings of the Second Workshop on Building Educational Applications Using NLP, Ann Arbor. EdAppsNLP 05, Association for Computational Linguistics, Stroudsburg, PA, USA, pp. 29–36.

Kao, A. & Poteet, S. (2005). Text Mining and Natural Language Processing: Introduction for the Special Issue. SIGKDD Explorations Newsletter, vol. 7, 1, pp. 1–2.

Kao, A. & Poteet, S.R. (2010). Natural Language Processing and Text Mining. Springer-Verlag, London.

Kaplan, A. & Haenlein, M. (2010). Users of the World, Unite! The Challenges and Opportunities of Social Media. Business Horizons, vol. 53, 1, pp. 59–68.

Keane, M., O'Brien, M. & Smyth, B. (2008). Are People Biased in Their Use of Search Engines? Communications of the ACM, vol. 51, 2, pp. 49–52.

Khazen, J.B. (1999). Censorship and State Control of the Press in the Arab World. The Harvard International Journal of Press/Politics, vol. 4, 3, pp. 87–92.

Kim, H.N., Rawashdeh, M. & El Saddik, A. (2011). Leveraging Collaborative Filtering to Tag-Based Personalized Search. In: Proceedings of the 19th International Conference on User Modeling, Adaption, and Personalization. UMAP'11, Springer-Verlag, Berlin, Heidelberg, pp. 195–206.

Knorr, E. (2003). 2004: The Year of Web Services. URL: http://www.cio.com/article/32050/2004_The_Year_of_Web_Services, accessed: May 3rd, 2012.

Kremerskothen, K. (2011). 6,000,000,000. URL: http://blog.flickr.net/en/2011/08/04/6000000000/, accessed: August 16, 2013.

Krums, J. (2009). Miracle of the Hudson. URL: `http://twitpic.com/135xa`, accessed: August 12, 2013.

Kutcher, A. (2013). Twitter Content Unit and Profile. URL: `https://twitter.com/aplusk`, accessed: September 25, 2013.

Langville, A.N. & Meyer, C.D. (2006). Google's PageRank and Beyond: The Science of Search Engine Rankings. Princeton University Press, Princeton, New Jersey.

Lelis, S. & Howes, A. (2011). Informing Decisions: How People Use Online Rating Information to Make Choices. In: Proceedings of the 2011 Annual Conference on Human Factors in Computing Systems. CHI '11, ACM, New York, pp. 2285–2294.

Lessig, L. (2001). The Future of Ideas: The Fate of the Commons in a Connected World. Random House, New York.

Li, H. (2011). Learning to Rank for Information Retrieval and Natural Language Processing. Morgan & Claypool, Toronto.

Lobo, S. (2013a). Facebook Profil. URL: `https://de-de.facebook.com/SaschaLobo`, accessed: September 26, 2013.

Lobo, S. (2013b). Google+ Profil. URL: `https://plus.google.com/+SaschaLobo/posts`, accessed: September 26, 2013.

Lovett, J. (2011). Social Media Metrics Secrets. Wiley, Indianapolis.

Macdonald, C., Santos, R.L., Ounis, I. & Soboroff, I. (2010). Blog Track Research at TREC. SIGIR Forum, vol. 44, pp. 58–75.

Manning, C.D., Raghavan, P. & Schütze, H. (2008). Introduction to Information Retrieval. Cambridge University Press, New York.

Marchionini, G. (2006). Exploratory Search: From Finding to Understanding. Communications of the ACM, vol. 49, pp. 41–46.

Marchionini, G. & Shneiderman, B. (1988). Finding Facts vs. Browsing Knowledge in Hypertext Systems. IEEE Computer, vol. 21, 1, pp. 70–80.

Meyer, B. (1997). Object-Oriented Software Construction. Prentice Hall, 2nd ed.

Mika, P. (2007). Social Networks and the Semantic Web. Springer Science+Business Media, New York.

Mishne, G. & Glance, N. (2006). Leave a Reply: An Analysis of Weblog Comments. In: Proceedings of the 3rd Annual Workshop on the Weblogging Ecosystem, Edinburgh. pp. 22–26.

Mooers, C.N. (1950). The Theory of Digital Handling of Non-Numerical Information and its Implications to Machine Economics. Zator, Boston, MA, USA.

Moturu, S. (2010). Quantifying the Trustworthiness of Social Media Content: Content Analysis for the Social Web. LAP Lambert Academic Publishing, Saarbrücken, Germany.

Moustafa, T. (2003). Law Versus the State: The Judicialization of Politics in Egypt. Law & Social Inquiry, vol. 28, 4, pp. 883–930.

Münker, S. (2009). Emergenz digitaler Öffentlichkeiten : die sozialen Medien im Web 2.0. Suhrkamp, Frankfurt am Main, Germany.

Nack, F. (2010). Social Compatibility. Multimedia, IEEE, vol. 17, 3, pp. 4–7.

Neilson, L.A. (2010). Boycott or Buycott? Understanding Political Consumerism. Journal of Consumer Behaviour, vol. 9, 3, pp. 214–227.

Oberquelle, H. (2002). Useware Design and Evolution: Bridging Social Thinking and Software Construction. In: Y. Dittrich, C. Floyd & R. Klischewski (Eds.), Social Thinking. MIT Press, Cambridge, MA, USA, pp. 391–408.

Opondo, M. (2013). Emerging Corporate Social Responsibility in Kenya's Cut Flower Industry. University of Nairobi. Department of Geography and Environmental Studies.

O'Reilly, T. (2005). What Is Web 2.0. URL: http://oreilly.com/ web2/archive/what-is-web-20.html, accessed: May 2, 2012.

Page, L., Brin, S., Motwani, R. & Winograd, T. (1998). The PageRank Citation Ranking: Bringing Order to the Web. Stanford Digital Library.

Pariser, E. (2011). The Filter Bubble: What the Internet is Hiding From You. Penguin, New York.

Peter (2013). Gottfrid i Medierna. URL: http://blog.brokep.com/, accessed: September 23, 2013.

Pier, K. (1991). Locator Technology in Distributed Systems: the Active Badge. In: Proceedings of the Conference on Organizational Computing Systems, Atlanta. COCS '91, ACM, New York, pp. 285–287.

Pöyry, E., Parvinen, P., Salo, J., Blakaj, H. & Tiainen, O. (2011). Online Information Search and Utilization of Electronic Word-of-Mouth. In: ICEC '11: Proceedings of the 13th International Conference on Electronic Commerce, Liverpool. ACM, New York, pp. 2:1–2:9.

Preston, J. (2011). Movement Began With Outrage and a Facebook Page that Gave It an Outlet. URL: http://www.nytimes. com /2012/02/19/books/review/how-an-egyptian-revolution -began-on-facebook.html?pagewanted=all&_r=0, accessed: August 13, 2013.

Raykar, V.C., Yu, S., Zhao, L.H., Valadez, G.H., Florin, C., Bogoni, L. & Moy, L. (2010). Learning from Crowds. Journal of Machine Learning Research, vol. 11, pp. 1297–1322.

Reichelt, J. (2013). Informationssuche und Online Word-of-Mouth. Springer, Wiesbaden, Germany.

Reilly, D., Dearman, D., Ha, V., Smith, I. & Inkpen, K. (2006). "Need to Know": Examining Information Need in Location Discourse. Pervasive Computing, pp. 33–49.

Richardson, M., Prakash, A. & Brill, E. (2006). Beyond PageRank: Machine Learning for Static Ranking. In: Proceedings of the 15th International Conference on World Wide Web, Edinburgh. ACM, New York, pp. 707–715.

Rogers, Y., Sharp, H. & Preece, J. (2011). Interaction Design: Beyond Human-Computer Interaction. Wiley, Sussex, 3rd ed.

RosesAreRed1207 (2012). My last iphone. URL: http://www.ciao.co.uk/Apple_iPhone_5_16GB__Review_6069358, accessed: September 26, 2013.

Safko, L. (2010). The Social Media Bible: Tactics, Tools, and Strategies for Business Success. Wiley, Hoboken, NJ, USA, 2nd ed.

Salton, G. & McGill, M. (1986). Introduction to Modern Information Retrieval. McGraw-Hill, New York.

Sanghvi, R. & Steinberg, A. (2010). F8 - Facebook Developer's Conference 2010. URL: http://www.livestream.com/f8conference, accessed: August 23, 2013.

Saracevic, T. (2007). Relevance: A review of the literature and a framework for thinking on the notion in information science. Part II: nature and manifestations of relevance. J. Am. Soc. Inf. Sci. Technol., vol. 58, 13, pp. 1915–1933.

Scellato, S., Noulas, A., Lambiotte, R. & Mascolo, C. (2011). Socio-Spatial Properties of Online Location-Based Social Networks. In: Proceedings of ICWSM, Barcelona. vol. 11, pp. 329–336.

Shen, X., Tan, B. & Zhai, C. (2005). Implicit User Modeling for Personalized Search. In: Proceedings of the 14th ACM International Conference on Information and Knowledge Management. CIKM '05, ACM, New York, pp. 824–831.

Shneiderman, B., Preece, J. & Pirolli, P. (2011). Realizing the Value of Social Media Requires Innovative Computing Research. Communications of the ACM, vol. 54, pp. 34–37.

Smith, E. Mackie, D. (2007). Social Psychology. Psychology Press Taylor & Friencis Group, New York, 3rd ed.

Solis, B. (2010). Engage: The Complete Guide for Brands and Businesses to Build, Cultivate, and Measure Success in the New Web. Wiley Publishing, Hoboken, NJ, USA.

Spiegel (2010). WeTab: Rezensionen vom Chef. URL: http://www.spiegel.de/fotostrecke/wetab-rezensionen-vom-chef-fotostrecke-60143.html, accessed: August 15, 2013.

Stanford (2013). Larry (Lawrence) Page. URL: http://infolab.stanford.edu/~page/, accessed: August 23, 2013.

Stelter, B. (2008). Finding Political News Online, the Young Pass It On. URL: http://www.nytimes.com/2008/03/27/us/politics/27voters.html, accessed: August 19, 2013.

Surowiecki, J. (2005). The Wisdom of Crowds. Abacus, London.

Tseng, S. & Fogg, B.J. (1999). Credibility and Computing Technology. Communications of the ACM, vol. 42, pp. 39–44.

Tumblr (2013a). About. URL: http://www.tumblr.com/about, accessed: August 16, 2013.

Tumblr (2013b). Follow the World's Creators. URL: http://www.tumblr.com/about, accessed: October 12, 2013.

United Nations (2012). The Millenium Development Goals Report 2012. United Nations, New York.

Van Rijsbergen, C. (1979). Information Retrieval. Butterworth, London.

Vargas, J.A. (2012). Spring Awakening, How an Egyptian Revolution Began on Facebook. URL: http://www.nytimes.com/2012/02/19/books/review/how-an-egyptian-revolution-began-on-facebook.html?pagewanted=all&_r=0, accessed: August 13, 2013.

Wanas, N., El-Saban, M., Ashour, H. & Ammar, W. (2008). Automatic Scoring of Online Discussion Posts. In: Proceedings of the 2nd ACM Workshop on Information Credibility on the Web. WICOW '08, ACM, New York, pp. 19–26.

Wang, H., He, X., Chang, M.W., Song, Y., White, R.W. & Chu, W. (2013). Personalized Ranking Model Adaptation for Web Search. In: Proceedings of the 36th International ACM SIGIR Conference on Research and Development in Information Retrieval. SIGIR '13, ACM, New York, pp. 323–332.

Wickre, K. (2013). Celebrating #Twitter7. URL: https://blog.twitter.com/2013/celebrating-twitter7, accessed: August 16, 2013.

Wikipedia (2013a). Social Media. URL: http://de.wikipedia.org/w/index.php?title=Social_Media&oldid=120839397, accessed: July 30, 2013.

Wikipedia (2013b). Social Media. URL: http://en.wikipedia.org/w/index.php?title=Social_media&oldid=566272789, accessed: July 30, 2013.

WordPress (2013). Categories. URL: http://en.support.word press.com/posts/categories, accessed: September 23, 2013.

Wulf, V., Misaki, K., Atam, M., Randall, D. & Rohde, M. (2013). 'On the Ground' in Sidi Bouzid: Investigating Social Media Use during the Tunisian Revolution. In: Proceedings of the 2013 Conference on Computer Supported Cooperative Work, San Antonio, TX, USA. CSCW '13, ACM, New York, pp. 1409–1418.

Youtube (2013). Statistics. URL: http://www.youtube.com/yt/press/en/statistics.html, accessed: August 16, 2013.

Yu, J., Low, K.H., Oran, A. & Jaillet, P. (2012). Hierarchical Bayesian Nonparametric Approach to Modeling and Learning the Wisdom of Crowds of Urban Traffic Route Planning Agents. In: Web Intelligence and Intelligent Agent Technology (WI-IAT), 2012

IEEE/WIC/ACM International Conferences. IEEE Computer Society, Washington, DC, USA, vol. 2 of WI-IAT '12, pp. 478–485.

Yu, J., Zha, Z.J., Wang, M. & Chua, T.S. (2011). Aspect Ranking: Identifying Important Product Aspects from Online Consumer Reviews. In: Proceedings of the 49th Annual Meeting of the Association for Computational Linguistics: Human Language Technologies, Portland. Association for Computational Linguistics, Stroudsburg, PA, USA, vol. 1 of HLT '11, pp. 1496–1505.

Zammit, V. (2008). Speakers' Corner — 50 Historical Pictures. Victor Zammit and Other Speakers at the Speakers' Corner, Domain Park, Sydney, Australia and at Speakers' Corner, Marble Arch, Hyde Park, England. URL: http://www.victorzammit.com/about/pictures.htm, accessed: October 17, 2013.

Zhang, L., Tang, L., Luo, P., Chen, E., Jiao, L., Wang, M. & Liu, G. (2012). Harnessing the Wisdom of the Crowds for Accurate Web Page Clipping. In: Proceedings of the 18th ACM SIGKDD International Conference on Knowledge Discovery and Data Mining, Beijing. KDD '12, ACM, New York, pp. 570–578.

Zhang, Z., Guo, C. & Goes, P. (2013). Product Comparison Networks for Competitive Analysis of Online Word-of-Mouth. ACM Transactions on Management Information Systems, vol. 3, 4, pp. 20:1–20:22.

Zhao, D. & Rosson, M.B. (2009). How and Why People Twitter: The Role that Micro-Blogging Plays in Informal Communication at Work. In: Proceedings of the ACM 2009 International Conference on Supporting Group Work, Sanibel Island. GROUP '09, ACM, New York, pp. 243–252.

Index